INDIAN EDUCATION

A CRITICAL VIEW

M. SEN GUPTA

ATLANTIC

PUBLISHERS & DISTRIBUTORS (P) LTD

ATLANTIC
PUBLISHERS & DISTRIBUTORS (P) LTD

7/22, Ansari Road, Darya Ganj, New Delhi
Tel.: +91-11-4077 5252, 2327 3880
E-mail: orders@atlanticbooks.com
Web: www.atlanticbooks.com

Published by Atlantic Publishers & Distributors (P) Ltd 2024

Printed & bound in India by Atlantic Print Services

Preface

Indian education in the post-independent India evolved from Mahatma Gandhi's mantra of self-dependence, self-sufficiency and learning by doing. Inspired by great Indian thinkers, the educational planners visualised mass education as a means of awakening the nation's conscience by building in self-reliance and dignity of the individual. The country's education system visualizes every Indian as a positive asset and a precious national resource. It intends to provide every individual an opportunity to discover and realize their inherent talents and potential by working with others towards national development. In the new millennium the system is faced with many hitherto unknown challenges. In order to carve out viable strategies, it is essential to take a critical look at its implementation.

The book in hand titled "Indian Education: A Critical View" is an honest effort in that direction. Divided into four sections, the book takes a comprehensive view encompassing issues and concerns, teacher, teacher education, the process of knowledge construction and the arduous task of skill development among the youth. Based on the varied and long experience of Prof. M. Sen Gupta, an established author discusses in the book, a number of eye-opening innovative experiments, futuristic visualizations, creation of research culture and policy imperatives. Each article has been so presented that the book has developed into a complete organic entity providing a vivid picture of different aspects of Indian Education.

Being in the field of education in various capacities for well over fifty years at national and international levels, Dr. Sen Gupta has presented a synthesis of his articles incorporating the latest information and in-depth analysis of each topic such that the book becomes useful to the students of education, teachers, teacher education and researchers.

The comprehensive coverage and experiential approach of the book in hand are distinct for its critical analysis, lucid presentation and up-to-date information. The book, therefore, will be a valuable addition to the libraries of teacher education colleges, universities departments, research and development institutions and innovative schools and colleges.

Prof A.V. Singh Madnawat
Formerly,
Head, Department of Psychology
Head, Department of Eduction
Director, PG School of Humanities
University of Rajasthan,
Jaipur-302004

Acknowledgement

The present book is a collection of my articles which appeared in newspapers, journals and magazines along with some latest ones. Hence, the thoughts presented here are an extension of my previous writings in books and journals wherein I have tried to provide further detailing and elaboration. In a constantly changing world, upgrading thoughts rather than just updating has become a necessity, and that has been my attempt here.

Each of the articles has been thoroughly revised and updated with the latest references, keeping a continuity with a basic thought process. The author gratefully acknowledges each source quoted in the text.

It is expected that this effort of wider dissemination of novel ideas and promising innovations will trigger fresh thinking on issues related to Indian Education.

M. Sen Gupta

Contents

SECTION 3
Vocational Education and Training

SECTION 4
Teaching and Learning

Introduction

With the advent of knowledge age, education systems globally are being reviewed and redesigned with emphasis on trans-disciplinary and multi-disciplinary perspectives, critical and creative thinking, problem-solving, machine learning and artificial intelligence. In India too in recent years due to the emergence of open and competitive global economy; reinforced by electronic communication technology the forces of globalization, modernization and urbanization started influencing the Indian psyche, the Indian market, Indian language, dress, culture, food habits, family system and even its strong educational traditions.

At this juncture, when these changes are transforming the age-old values, cultural and management practices, creating new types of jobs, revolutionizing the industry, business and service sector processes; it is impossible to continue with the traditional education model. It is time that some key aspects of the existing system are critically viewed and judged to align it with the new societal demands with a view to benefit from the emerging opportunities and skillfully face the twenty-first century challenges.

The book in hand is an honest and impartial effort in that direction. Divided into four Sections namely 'Issues and Concerns', 'Teacher and Teacher Education', 'Vocational Education and Training' and 'Teaching and Learning', it is a scholarly treatise that probes deep into each aspect, analyses it from all possible angles, synthesizes these in a holistic perspective and gives a futuristic and suggestive paradigm.

Section 1 focuses on establishing relevance of present day education to meet the needs of a vibrant democracy, changing expectations of the world of work, India's spiritual traditions, gender equality and the role of media. Teacher and Teacher Education are the backbone of any education system. Section 2 makes a critical appraisal of the product and processes, presents experiments and innovative experiences in order to propose a futuristic model. Section 3 deals with the most essential but so far elusive concept of vocational education and training. Carefully selected topics in each Section throw light on its present status and future possibilities. Each one has been meticulously analysed to arrive at an implementable model based on author's rich experience in the field. Finally, the last Section answers the question 'How it is to be done'. The approach here is experiential, realistic, innovative and keeping in view the viability along with refinement.

Instead of following a theoretical orientation the book emphasizes on integration of theory and practice fortified by exploration, experimentation and innovation. Language throughout has been kept simple so that students, teachers, teacher educators and researchers at every level can easily understand and apply the innovative ideas in their respective institutions. It is hoped that the material given in the book will be particularly useful to those who are engaged in planning, research and executing educational projects and programmes. The book will definitely be a valuable addition to the libraries of teacher education institutions, university departments of education, research and development institutions and innovative schools and colleges.

Bringing out the book in the present form could not have been possible without the divine inspiration and blessings. Further, I thank my wife Shaon, my two sons Satyajit and Shivaji, daughters-in-law Sohini and Amrita who willingly cooperated in discussions. I shall be failing in my duty if I do not mention my grandsons Saarthak, Rishaan and granddaughter Aanya who allowed me to complete the job in time. Last but not the least I am thankful to Atlantic Publishers and Distributors (P) Ltd. for their quick and positive response in getting the book published.

A look at the diversified content will indicate that the book is not just yet another book on the subject but stands distinct for its professional and analytical approach, intelligent presentation, clear, concise and lucid language along with experiential experimentations and innovations. The author has intelligently used his rich experience to make the book objective, authentic and up-to-date. Students pursuing courses in Education and particularly Teacher Education like B.Ed., M.Ed., B.Sc.-B.Ed., and B.A.-B.Ed. will find the book refreshing, novel in content and enriching. Besides, the book will be of immense use to the teacher Educators and researchers due to its intensive analytical approach, research orientation and contemporary focus.

M. Sen Gupta

Section 1
Issues and Concerns

1

Education Relevant to Independent India: Need for Policy Initiatives

The British Legacy

Every debate till date on relevance, effectiveness and appropriateness of Indian educational system invariably begins by blaming the British education system that we inherited. But we conveniently forget the basic tenet that any country achieving independence from a colonial power must gradually develop an education system relevant to its cultural and developmental needs on a priority basis for empowering its citizens to be creators of their own destinies. This particularly becomes essential for preserving, promoting and expressing its unique socio-cultural identity. Such empowerment will ensure that the newly independent democratic country committed to parliamentary democracy is able to meet the challenges of changing times. This is because once the colonial rulers leave, the power shifts from rulers to the ruled.

India adopted democratic polity with a promise to establish a welfare state for the people and create an egalitarian society based on democratic ideals, social justice, individual liberty, equity and equality without any form of discrimination of caste, colour, creed or sex. In a democracy, it is the people—their creativity and independent thinking who play a crucial role since a human being is the greatest asset in such a people-driven democratic set-up. In a parliamentary democracy like India, it is the elected representatives of the people who formulate, plan, organise, innovate and implement pro-people policies and programmes.

Although the country adopted its constitution after independence, it did not care to reconstruct its education system in the changed political reality. Instead, it chose to continue with the existing colonial system fashioned by Macaulay. Thus, in place of producing innovators, leaders and creators, the education system continued to be subservient to the political bosses and its bureaucratic work culture. Such a system undoubtedly provided much-needed continuity but failed to appreciate the changing roles and responsibilities of the people in a nascent democracy. Instead of evolving an education system in line with the Indian geo-political requirements, the educational planners preferred to introduce curricular reforms in a piecemeal manner over the years. Such transformational efforts through commissions and committees, constituted from time to time, proved to be a patchwork on the basic colonial structure. This could have been avoided if, alternatively, they had revisited, reconceptualised and reimagined the entire approach, methodology, processes, outputs and outcomes of education in a holistic manner. It is essential to give a lead to the scientific and technological advancements to promote its strong socio-cultural and educational heritage and continue its great spiritual legacy. However, driven by the strong feeling of nationalism and new-found enthusiasm to make a place within the communion of countries, the people of India worked wholeheartedly all these years to accelerate the country's pace of development. There is no denying of the fact that in the last 70 years, the country has taken great strides in every field. Today, we are politically and economically stronger than ever before. But unfortunately, many undesirable customs, values and norms of traditional society are still very much alive in the contemporary Indian society. A number of communities, even today, remain largely traditional and entangled in age-old social evils. History tells us that the golden era of *Bharat* was lost mainly due to fissiparous tendencies, lack of social cohesion, evils of class, caste, gender discrimination and selfish ambitions. The Independence movement could make successful inroads simply because it effectively highlighted Indian identity, infused pride in Indian goods and strengthened Indian cultural and religious customs and traditions, which transformed into strength, so essential to throw the mighty British out.

With the advent of an open and competitive global economy reinforced by electronic communication technology, the forces of globalisation strongly and systematically invaded the Indian psyche, the Indian market, Indian language, dress, culture, food habits, family system and even our strong Indian educational traditions. The question that emerges is 'how to fight this cultural invasion'? Yet another disturbing trend emerged when in its race to make easy bucks, the society became subservient to developed economies. Creativity, innovation and independent thinking along with entrepreneurial culture were the biggest causalities due to this undesirable trend.

It was, therefore, absolutely necessary to start a countrywide debate just after independence on important issues like 'What is our vision of the next generation of Indian citizens? How to create and strengthen Indian identity? How to revive the creative entrepreneurial culture of India? How to evolve an educational policy to transform the education system such that it is capable of instilling in its citizens, originality in thinking and courage to invent and innovate? And how to inculcate in them faith and pride in Indian educational and spiritual traditions?' The present-day education system and its curriculum having strong western ideological flavours have led people to pursue materialism with total disregard for life values like tolerance, mutual trust, unity in diversity, peaceful living, the divinity of humankind and respect for all forms of life and environment. This has resulted in a culture of violence by creating fear through terror and distrust among fellow human beings. Society is facing violence in its most primitive form. There is a definite trend towards dissatisfaction and a craving for more material comforts. In the absence of faith and spiritual satisfaction, social tensions are giving an impetus to suicidal tendencies.

Emergence of a New Philosophy

It was Gandhi, the father of the nation, who, by his farsightedness and his human-centric approach to life, for the first time realised the need for a robust native education system based on advancing indigenous craftsmanship, the mantra of self-sufficiency and learning by doing. He advocated mother tongue/regional language as the medium of instruction. To him, education was 'Drawing out of the best in man—body, mind and spirit'. Gandhi was of the firm view that education must lead to a balanced development of an individual—physical, intellectual and spiritual, and that in any education process, these developments must go hand in hand.

Gandhian philosophy of education believed in harmonious development of the head, hand and heart. He was aware of the fact that purely intellectual or heavily material culture bears in its heart the seeds of death. A viable alternative lies in the synthesis of the two aspects of human life, namely material and spiritual. It requires a fresh philosophy of education based on Eastern wisdom, characterised by self-realisation, self-actualisation, inner tranquillity and spiritual upliftment. This of course, will have to be reinforced by Western preference for development orientation through appropriate technology for the common good. Education must strengthen human values and faith in the divinity of soul and lead the new generation to higher ideals. Selfless service to humanity, commitment to social justice, sustainable development and an Indian lifestyle based on faith and satisfaction, detachment and minimum needs should be the guiding principles in this context.

Therefore, the endeavour should be to give the nation a balanced and holistic education system to ensure for its citizens both material and spiritual well-being. But alas! The well-meaning and procontextual system of basic education was phased out unceremoniously by those who were the products of the British education system. If it was given a fair trial and progressively transformed as per needs of the day, it could have developed into an alternative education system founded on Indian soil and nurtured by the Indian way of thinking.

Contemporary Educational Concerns

A. Revitalising Universities

India is a land of diversities. Universities are no exception. Administratively, there are central, state, private and deemed universities. There are specialised universities like agricultural universities, technological universities, universities of teacher education and rural universities. Open universities offer ODL courses. The emergence of skill universities in some states is a fairly recent development. Also, with the focus to boost skill development, skill up-gradation and vocational education, many universities have restructured their courses to accommodate vocational elements. Introduction of bachelor of vocational education courses in selected colleges has added a new dimension. Sooner or later, there is likely to be a demand for 'vocational universities', which will affiliate vocational colleges and institutes, carry out research and development work on emerging vocational areas and help in creating a cadre of vocational educators for the post-secondary stage. The community colleges movement in India is suffering in the absence of vocational universities that can give them the much-needed affiliation.

Incidentally, affiliating universities today are functioning like parallel regulatory bodies. They, in addition to conducting external examinations, are busy enforcing their own regulations to fetch extra finances and to show their brute authority. Many of these regulations are only duplicating the efforts of statutory regulatory or accreditation bodies. As highly specialised academic universities, they should in fact show their scholarly authority. Their main focus should be on raising the quality of the affiliated colleges and ensuring holistic educational outcomes by providing them with innovative academic leadership. Training and retraining of their faculty through University Academic Staff Colleges and reaching out to the colleges with sponsored seminars, conferences and specialised demonstrations on emerging or advanced issues are only a few examples in this context. Frequent faculty exchange between universities and colleges can create an academic fraternity based on equality and teamwork.

Universities with the best resources and brains at their disposal should form specialised research groups to take up original research work at the frontiers of knowledge for furthering the cause of human welfare. If need be they should delegate PG and Ph.D. research work to affiliated colleges and concentrate on path-breaking researches in the Indian cultural context. Of course, government restrictions on recruitment to attract the best of talents.

B. Academic Autonomy to Private Initiatives

Another area of concern is the stranglehold of the government on private and self-financing initiatives at every possible point, thereby robbing them of innovations, excellence and initiatives. The very reasons why government institutions are not able to perform have now percolated down to private institutions. One can understand the need for major government guidelines to be adhered to by these institutions, but frequent restrictions and interventions by government departments not for furthering any academic purpose but to show their authority is shaking the roots of these institutions. Unscrupulous elements in government authorities are almost strangling them to the extent of demotivating the management to serve the needy. As a matter of fact, the best of such private initiatives need to be encouraged, rewarded and enriched for exemplary results. Government should instead give grant-in-aid to deserving self-financing institutions for conducting research, taking up innovations and supporting quality education.

Many well-meaning private initiatives by efficient and honest persons are struggling due to financial crunch and unnecessary financial demands by unscrupulous government servants. The private and self-financing institutions based on their accreditation status should receive subsidies, incentives and lump sum financial assistance to help them work towards excellence, particularly in rural and less developed areas. One must not forget that private providers came into being because the government machinery failed to fulfil social commitments.

C. Medium of Instruction

Creativity requires a dream, along with perseverance and divergent thinking abilities to fulfil that dream. For children, creative dreaming requires thinking in 'dream language'. Unfortunately, these days in the name of globalisation, the dream language propounded by Dr. Triguna Sen has been relegated to the back seat. More and more schools, both government and private, are teaching every subject in English language, right from class 1, in the name of globalisation . They are, oblivious of the fact that majority of the children are not at all comfortable with this foreign language and cannot grasp the soul of the subject being taught as they do not understand the language well. So how are they going to understand what teachers are teaching? Consequently, they learn by rote and reproduce them verbatim in examinations. The system thus hardly produces creative, imaginative or independent-thinking people.

The author has seen numerous such classrooms in urban, semi-urban and rural areas. The situation becomes bad to worse as we move from urban to rural, from middle-class social strata to disadvantaged children from slums and low-income families. This is particularly true at the elementary level. Boys and girls are literally becoming parrots in human form, devoid of any constructive or creative abilities. Every educational thinker has stressed the need for the mother tongue or the regional language as the medium of instruction to make learning a joyful and creative experience for children. It is only through the medium of mother tongue or regional language that these children will be able to relate new knowledge to the previous knowledge, thereby constructing their own knowledge and attaining conceptual clarity.

The idea is not to discourage the learning of English as a lingua franca in a globalised world. Due emphasis to English language particularly for meaningful communication is a must. Students do require a good command over English as a communicative language to take advantage of the rich literature, especially in science, technology and engineering, available globally and to communicate freely with the outer world. But no useful purpose is served by imposing English as medium of instruction for all subjects. The latter strategy is against the psycho-social principles of learning and thinking by the child at that age. Learning every subject by rote year after year without reflecting and understanding, negates the very purpose of education, namely developing the thought process, encouraging innovation and arousing curiosity. As regards to developing proficiency in English in terms of reading, writing and communicating, children can effectively do so through the systematic and sustained study of that language by well-trained teachers using modern techniques and functional language laboratories.

One can hardly give any scientific justification for stultifying the thinking capacity of children by imposing a foreign language as medium of instruction. This also has larger cultural ramifications. People, in general, need to be educated to differentiate between the role of English as the medium of instruction and gaining business proficiency in English as an international language. Today every career requires functional language specific to that specialised field. Hardly any purpose is served by teaching history, geography, civics, environmental science, etc., in English, especially at the primary and upper primary stages.

D. Lack of Entrepreneurial Culture

Developing an entrepreneurial culture is indispensable for the process of encouraging youths to go for self-employment and for giving a boost to creation of wealth and further employment. In a predominantly young nation like India, a spirit of entrepreneurship and the urge for self-employment requires to be infused, nurtured and developed in learners on a priority basis right from the beginning. A large number of trainers will have to be systematically trained with the knowledge of entrepreneurial qualities, strategies for their development and other necessary requirements for starting a small-scale venture with a modest investment of financial and other resources. Further, they will have to be reoriented at regular intervals in tune with the market demands and availability of opportunities and support facilities.

It is hardly necessary to emphasise that the pace of economic progress of a country and the rate of development of its economy, to a great extent, depend upon entrepreneurial culture and self-employment initiatives of its people. A self-employment venture in long run triggers a number of economic activities in the vicinity such as construction of roads, provision of electricity, means of transport and communication, postal, banking and other services. Thus, gradually the entrepreneurial initiative starts a chain of activities that generates many opportunities for employment. In fact, employment generation through self-employment initiatives in small-scale industries or small businesses is cheaper than through wage employment in offices or large establishments.

It is commonly observed that young people due to their academic orientation choose the path of least resistance and tend to opt for a wage-earning career. It is our society that encourages the spread of such orientation. It is the family and the school that largely implant the qualities of conformity and compliance considered instrumental in nurturing service attitude. Unfortunately, the entrepreneurial qualities of creativity, risk taking, perseverance, problem-solving and innovativeness are not very much encouraged. This is the reason why such qualities that are required for an entrepreneurial career remain dormant or are found lacking in the youth.

As a matter of fact, many opportunities exist in the society, but one has to be sensitive enough to benefit from them. Majority of the people are able to appreciate only the apparent and traditional openings for earning. While a potential entrepreneur, besides sensing the opportunity, will develop within himself capabilities for selecting suitable and viable projects, formulating project reports, arranging for land and machinery, availing facilities and resources, and starting an entrepreneurial career instead. Creativity is embedded in the entrepreneurial culture. An entrepreneur generates wealth, introduces new firms, products or marketing strategies and innovates value-addition techniques. He explores the market and social activities, experiments with new products or methods, and even invents new products, methods, tools, equipment or techniques. Vision and creativity are the parts of a problem-solving-oriented decision-making processes. The entrepreneur always tries to overcome specific barriers of creativity like fear of failure, intolerance of ambiguity and prematurely trying out new ideas.

An innovative entrepreneur is imaginative, resourceful, persistent and self-confident. A new venture takes shape particularly because of the inner urge experienced by the entrepreneur to be innovative and creative. In today's world creativity and innovation have gained utmost significance as a new competitive differentiator. Therefore, our education policymakers should design a system to make our children successful entrepreneurs rather than opting en masse for salaried jobs.

E. Traditional Model of Teacher Training

Teacher education as it is being practiced in colleges of education today, largely involves sermonising on idealistic lines. The curriculum transaction is mostly theoretical, bookish and exam oriented—most of the time far from contemporary school realities. The training of teachers and teacher educators is utterly inadequate, especially in the affective domain. The student teachers hardly develop the desirable attitudes, values and art of human relationships. The process of teacher education is skewed towards facts and information emanating from secondary sources. Practical and pragmatic aspects of present-day human society and its dynamics are neither discussed nor experienced. Teaching-learning largely revolves around a set syllabus, a textbook and the examination structure. It is neither outcome based nor holistic in its approach.

In the emerging knowledge society, the content and process of teacher education have to strike a well-proportioned balance between the theoretical and practical, technological and human inputs, global and local requirements, modern and traditional, competition and cooperation, subjective and objective, as well as between philosophical, psychological and investigative. It has to transform itself into a process that is practical in its approach, research-based in its transactions, value-based in its outlook and 'learning to learn' as its motto.

Today, the need is also being felt for specialised content cum methodology oriented teacher education programmes of longer duration for senior secondary stage, vocational education and training, computer education, educational technology, engineering education and management education. There is, therefore, a need to have a comprehensive policy of teacher education in the country. A number of teacher education universities have since been established. It is time that the university system comes forward with new models of teacher education to meet the newer avenues being generated by the knowledge society of tomorrow. The boundaries of teacher education have to be extended by bringing in more and more specialisations while retaining the human aspects that a physically present teacher brings to the classroom.

Conclusion

At this point of time, when the country is at the threshold of socio-economic transformation due to knowledge-based digital technology, the education planners should project a vision of the future clearly spelling out the human capacities and competencies to be promoted. Simultaneously it should suggest measures to preserve Indian identity and probe deeper into Indian wisdom and its spiritualism, thereby moving towards a synthesis between Indian and Western thoughts to arrive at a progressive system that should draw its nutrition from Indian soil. Such a synthesis has become particularly pertinent because of prevailing conflicts and contradictions due to the forces of globalisation on the one hand and local cultural identity on the other. The education system in emerging India must try to bridge the gap between these opposing forces to arrive at social harmony and individual satisfaction.

2

Decision-Making in Independent India

In British India, the privilege of taking decisions was with the colonial power. Understandably, pre-independence administrators took decisions as per the demands and requirements of the then colonial system. Consequently, they created an educational system, often called the Macaulay system, that basically propagated English language and culture. They made the natives to blindly submit to the authority and carry out their orders faithfully. Needless to mention that they succeeded remarkably in their endeavour to create a population which was Indian in flesh and blood but became English in thought and culture. They prepared Indians to work as cog in the machine, devoid of creativity, imagination or entrepreneurship.

With independence, however, the centre of power changed and so did the role of the masses in the changed political scenario. The natives now had to hold the reins of government. They no longer had to wait for orders and directions from the top. Democracy bestowed rights and responsibilities to every individual. They were now supposed to influence policy decisions and also wholeheartedly contribute to implement them in a democratic polity. This sudden change of role obviously required a complete change in outlook, process and direction of thinking. It required the creation of a whole infrastructure of the decision-making culture suitable to a free nation which was expected to provide leadership worth emulating by the smaller nations in the region.

Traditional Decision-Making

At this juncture, it would be useful to remember that decision-making is a problem-solving process. Efficient and effective decision-making requires courage, innovativeness and creativity on the part of the person taking decisions. If the decision taken has to break new grounds, give new directions and accelerate the pace of development, it would require specific behavioural and other inputs and also multiple strategies. Education being a powerful agent of behavioural change, the question that becomes most significant is: 'Have we been able to change the colonial education system into a more responsive education system suited to the needs of an independent democratic nation in which a questioning attitude replaces abject acceptance, divergent and lateral thinking are given their duc share along with rational and convergent thinking, and perpetuation of status quo is replaced by innovative ideas and off-the-track decision-making?' The answer is obviously negative.

As of today, the persons occupying decision-making positions in the country are the products of post-independence education system. Unfortunately, their decision-making capabilities are not only slow and not driven by farsightedness but also in the long run, prove to be far from satisfactory. The prevailing work culture considers a person successful and fit for promotion if they follow the stale statutory rules faithfully, are able to write long but inconclusive notes that move from one seat to another at a snail's pace—the cumbersome process being followed mainly to avoid any unpleasant consequences; however, at the end achieving nothing except maintaining the status quo. There is hardly any point of deviation or an element of risk-taking in the process of decision-making. Further, there are instances when ad-hoc decisions have been taken without tackling the larger problems or assessing long-term consequences. Due to such decisions made at different points in time and at different levels, we find that the teaching community today stands totally fragmented and divided. The permanent teaching cadre is in jeopardy. There are shiksha karmis, shiksha mitra, guru ji, part-time teachers, contract teachers, para-teachers, guest teachers and so on. Absence of full-time teachers will have long-term adverse effects in the system.

Good decision-making should be governed by the reasoning as to how useful the outcome or impact of the decision will be on the organisation or the employees. What will be the consequences of the decision made in terms of higher profits, greater productivity or better efficiency? Instead, present-day decision-makers in public institutions and offices are governed by stale rules, avoiding audit objections, fear of RTI and inclinations of the higher up. They just tend to solve an immediate problem to save the current situation before they move to greener pastures.

Need for Change

As a matter of fact, the system is still largely run by the *babus* educated in the colonial pattern, trained by the system to suspect everything and everyone, thereby ruthlessly steamrolling any initiative and innovation in the process. If free India intends/wants to compete and succeed in a global economy, it cannot continue to perpetuate the system which breeds indecision and a callous attitude. Such a system can never encourage initiative, allow innovations, sustain excellence or face any worthwhile challenge.

Besides, in this system, one gets isolated or even pushed out if one dares to show initiative and risk-taking behaviour. Acceptance and rewards, if any, are reserved for those who maintain the system without venturing into new directions, novel pathways or developing any efficient strategy. It is perhaps time that the system takes stock of the situation and, without losing any more time, moves towards an aggressive, innovative and creative decision-making process in place of signature-based, file-oriented and caste/religion-driven decision-making. Indecision indicates an individual's inability to make particular decision at an appropriate time; the trait of indecisiveness represents an acquired personal characteristics, which the individual displays frequently in the course of making decisions. Decision is actually a judgment and is rarely a choice between right or wrong. At best, it is a choice between 'almost right' and 'almost wrong'.

Appropriate Decision-Making

Quick and appropriate decision-making is an important component of organisational behaviour of an individual. Decision-making occurs as a reaction to a problem. Whenever there exists a discrepancy between current state of affairs and some desired state, there is a need to consider alternative courses of action to arrive at a decision. The innovative decision-maker must have the ability to generate multitude of hypotheses or ask many questions which direct them to explore constructive measures for changing or correcting perceived inadequacies. He or she tends to be more autonomous than others, puts a premium on independence and freedom and is likely to avoid situations in which others try to dominate or coerce them. Creative personality is perceptually 'open'.

Unfortunately, our day-to-day culture, education system, curriculum, methods of teaching, instructional technology and textbooks are not in consonance with the development of this human asset. Our curriculum offerings and textbooks pay homage to the same God of continuity and conformity and emphasise upon convergent abilities at the cost of divergent abilities, independent thinking and independent judgment. There is, therefore, an urgent need to bring about curriculum innovations in schools and colleges such that our policymakers, top-level administrators and managers are able to view problems from different vintage points and spin-off along the tangent of risk-taking and uncertainty rather than perpetuating the circle of conformity and orthodoxy.

3
Nurturing Potential Creativity

Introduction

Schools and colleges these days are invariably claiming that they are immersed in developing creativity and innovation among their students. However, it is doubtful how much they really appreciate or understand these two concepts and their functional or practical significance. Most of the time, they use the words as rhetoric. It will not be an exaggeration to say that in most cases it is nothing but paying lip service to the buzz words. A deeper probe into their day-to-day routine and curriculum will reveal that most, schools follow the traditional curricular practices, which, as we know, are devoid of thrill, joy and passion for learning. Schools need to keep themselves abreast of the knowledge about new developments, new ideas, and novel creations emerging in the world of education.

Creativity is not just adding or enriching the curriculum, but it is also promoting a way of thinking to generate new ideas and new products that are essential for a global workforce in this age of knowledge and artificial intelligence. More the creativity gap, less relevant the curriculum becomes. But what exactly is creativity? Creativity can be understood as a cluster of skills. These cognitive skills are articulated to produce original, unusual and valuable ideas which are useful to mankind.

Creative teachers use imaginative methods and approaches to learning. Their ultimate aim is to make learning much more interesting, exciting and effective. Creativity is in all of us. There are umpteen number of ways in which one can express their creativity. Experts feel that creativity is multidimensional in nature and thus is composed of a set of skills and attitudes within a person. Sensing new problems, redefining or re-looking at existing problems from entirely different angles, taking calculated risk, seeking complexity and tolerating ambiguity are some important characteristics of a creative person. Creativity and divergent thinking skills lead to success in school on the one hand, and enable the future workforce to solve emerging problems with courage and imagination on the other.

Lifelong Learning

In the knowledge age, machines are designed to undertake routine tasks. Computers and other similar gadgets yield almost all needed information. Hence, students need to be independent learners and be ready to learn throughout life because in the changing occupational world they will have to constantly adapt and adjust to new situations, innovate new techniques, ideas, and products, and solve hitherto unknown problems in the workplace.

In the revised Bloom's Taxonomy, 'creating' is the highest educational objective to be achieved. On reaching this stage, students will be able to identify and connect broad patterns emerging out of different disciplines, thus enabling inter-disciplinary studies. With the achievement of this objective, students develop a deeper understanding of the problems and are able to solve them and explore multiple links and options following enquiry approach of learning. A safe and secure learning environment that allows autonomy and risk-taking ability, facilitates expression of creativity. Therefore, it is the teacher's duty to provide the learner a play-oriented, joyful, open and supportive environment wherein the voices of the learner is heard and valued.

Nurturing Creativity in Students

Facilitating creative thinking among students should be the aim of all teachers in this knowledge age. A dynamic and free learning environment encourages every students to satisfy their curiosity in their own peculiar way. The teacher guides the learner to develop and sharpen their abilities and talents and pursue interests to their best advantage. Teachers encourage students to go dashing off in new directions. Learners are exposed to questioning and exploration. Potential of creativity exists in everyone. The notion that only genius or exceptional people are capable of creativity is no longer valid. Even the notion of one IQ has been demolished by Gardner's theory of multiple intelligences. Creativity requires proper atmosphere and nurturing for its full development. Hence, let students take initiative, explore problems, analyse data and find solutions. The basic idea is to train their intellect to enable them to adjust and re-adjust in the fast-changing world.

In a classroom/school situation, teachers can promote and nurture creativity in a variety of ways. Following are some simple ways that can be tried in day-to-day interactions with students.

- As said earlier, creative learning requires creation of a learning environment characterised by acceptance, compassion and permissiveness to the extent that students are allowed to even commit mistakes and learn from them. They are given enough autonomy to explore, experiment and learn from their own experiences.
- Provide ample opportunities for creating new ideas, new ways of doing things, designing new and useful gadgets, imagining situations or stories, making estimations, innovating new projects and for solving variety of problems by exploring as many different solutions as possible.
- Use a variety of teaching strategies that promote creative thinking. Pose open-ended questions and problems, which can have more than one possible answer or solution. Let students value each solution to arrive at the most acceptable or effective one. They can work on open-ended projects that encourage divergent thinking and give enough opportunities to arrive at probable solutions. Creative teaching methods like

brainstorming, attribute listing, bionics or synectics can also be tried. The teacher may use different ways of introducing the lesson, presenting the lesson or evaluating the outcomes.

- Identify the students showing unusual behaviour. Study their behaviour carefully for any creative expression. Maybe their answers or solutions show independence of thinking or some new spark. If so, try to channelise their behaviour towards creative problem-solving or bringing in them originality of thought and action.
- Creativity is hard to come by. As is often said, 99 percent perspiration leads to 1 percent inspiration. Hence, make the students understand that it takes much effort to arrive at a satisfactory solution while working on a project since creative problem-solving requires imagining and re-imagining several times.
- Through various facts and examples, let the students appreciate how creativity gets manifested and finds expression in the form of creative products and processes around them.
- Encourage autonomy. Don't let yourself be the arbiter of what 'good' work is. Instead, give feedback that encourages self-assessment and independence.
- Assignments to be given to students can be so designed that they are required to create, design, plan or invent something by using their imagination. Similarly, in assignments, problems may be so posed that they have the freedom to present as many solutions as possible.
- Let the students take up activities like visual riddles. These riddles in the form of drawings or paintings can have a wide range of interpretations that will enable students to use their creative thinking abilities. The idea is to stimulate divergent thinking on the part of the students by giving as many different interpretations as possible. Similarly, when students are asked to complete a story, prepare a cartoon on a given concept,

give the unusual ending of an event or quickly give their viewpoints on a situation, their minds are trained to think in a variety of ways. Practising creative thinking in this manner can go a long way in preparing students to be productive in a creative and innovative manner.

- There are students who are not inherently aware of their potential creativity. Teachers can enable them to explore their creative competence by giving them open-ended assignments along with those related to traditional academic competence. Provide students feedback on their creativity. When evaluation specifically indicates the off-the-cuff achievements of students, they get motivated and thus develop a self-concept in which creativity is embedded to play an important role.

Facilitating creativity among students should be the aim of all teachers in this knowledge age. Every student, in their own way, can satisfy their curiosity, develop their abilities and talents and pursue their interests to their best advantage.

Nurturing Creativity in Teachers

Just as nurturing creativity in students is the duty of the teacher, similarly teachers too need to cultivate and nurture their own creativity. Only creative teachers can trigger creativity in students. It is these creative teachers who are open to new challenges in a classroom situation and are found to be better equipped to deal with them with confidence. These teachers reinvent their own potential to successfully address the individual differences amongst students. This is done by adopting new teaching styles or different strategies of teaching. Teaching creatively requires the 'right' set of skills and appropriate dispositions. To be creative, teachers should be duly motivated, have a positive attitude towards divergent thinking abilities and be ready to use innovative approaches and strategies. Some possible ways to do this are described in the following section.

It is the general feeling that teacher educators in teacher education institutions resort to more of telling and sermonising rather than doing and practically implementing. Most of the pedagogical teaching in a classroom situation deals with generalities. There is much less emphasis on practice for developing specific skills hands-on. Consequently, there is hardly any effective feedback. Hence, teacher education today is in urgent need of reform.

It is necessary to ensure that teacher behaviour is compatible with the contemporary philosophy of education and the changing needs of society. The planners must realise the changed societal and professional needs of teachers in this age of knowledge and artificial intelligence. Teacher education curriculum must include creative teaching-learning strategies, innovative ways of learning and inculcating problem-solving disposition. Today, teachers find themselves in a context that is characterised by sweeping social and technological change. There is an explosion of knowledge in almost every field of inquiry. Population mobility and population explosion are happening at an accelerated rate. The character of modern life is increasingly becoming more complex. Therefore, the design of teacher education curriculum must take a fresh look at the needs of our pre-service and in-service teachers. Decision regarding reforms in teacher education in the contemporary world should no longer be taken based on customs, traditions and intuition. It should instead take cognizance of the important influences upon the nature of learning opportunities and on the nature of content and methods involved in the education of teachers. In other words, the objectives of teacher education programmes need to be laid out freshly, taking into consideration the changed societal and professional needs of teachers.

Developing Creativity in Teachers

A deeper insight into the educational practices in our classrooms today will reveal that in the content and process of education from primary through secondary, right up to the college stage, emphasis is laid on giving the learner readymade knowledge, systematically and neatly organised in the form of rigid syllabus, textbooks and testing techniques. The entire syllabus is prescribed, and the teacher is required to follow it faithfully. Schooling has become a routine exercise of imparting and receiving knowledge. It transforms the learner into a good receiver of knowledge, a good memoriser ready to produce set answers to given problems. The learner, therefore, hardly develops the ability to ask thought-provoking questions. They lack the potential of producing novel ideas or using their imagination for creating something exciting to take the society a step forward. At this stage, it is important to remember that creative thinking abilities can be developed in varying degrees among different individuals through an imaginatively planned and organised instruction.

Creative teachers are independent in their thinking and judgment not partisan or dogmatic. They are flexible, open to new ideas, not at all worried about opposition or criticism and quite imaginative and persistent. In order to be creative, the teachers can develop these qualities in themselves by following some simple steps. These may be described as:

1. Be knowledgeable

The teacher has to be knowledgeable. For this, they should:

- Read every type of available reading material, including books, e-books, journals, magazines, newspapers, research articles and so on
- Attend training courses, orientation and refresher courses
- Take online courses, solve quizzes and read extensively the papers originating from international sources
- Use online resources, websites, portals and other e-learning platforms
- Attend university refresher programmes, seminars and conferences
- Try some artistic hobbies such as playing a musical instrument or following a theatre course
- Use songs, games and participatory strategies in the classroom

- Improve your language and pronunciation, communication skills and interpersonal qualities.

2. Connect with creative and innovative people

Connecting with other teachers and discussing with colleagues and friends on various issues open new horizons of thinking. One may get inspired by good orators, good speakers and promising writers. One can join a teacher's association, listen to talks, audio and video presentations and participate in workshops and seminars either offline or online. These develop a desire to imitate them or even do better. Outstanding teachers inspire others to improve their teaching practices.

3. Collect, organise and use better teaching ideas

Collect and organise new, promising and innovative teaching ideas. You can also devise your own teaching strategies and aids by using your ingenuity. Experiment with them at appropriate points in your teaching. As you elaborate, adapt and experiment, your creativity will flourish. New ideas can be collected online as well. You can also share your ideas online or through social media platforms.

4. Share your knowledge and learning

Knowledge is a wealth that increases with sharing by mutual interactions. One can lead a session, discuss new topics, present some innovation or share experiences with peers. Your ideas may sometimes be abstract but try to express them in a lucid and convincing manner. Many a times, these sharing moments turn out to be great learning opportunities for the contributors themselves. Allow open discussion on your presentation. Accept any criticism and be open to change.

There may be other ways of sharing ideas like starting a journal, writing articles or blogs. In either case, when new ideas of teaching are described, they generate further conversations, which in turn stimulate more ideas thereby facilitating creative teaching.

5. Remove the blocks to creative thinking

While there are people who are not afraid to express their creative potential, there are others who are not sure of their capabilities and therefore, hesitate to express their creativity and imagination. Their creative talents may thus remain hidden. As rightly said, creativity is in every one of us, but the skills and abilities will vary from person to person. High self-esteem and a positive self-concept go a long way in facilitating creative expression.

6. Practise creativity

To keep the spark of creativity alive, regular practice is essential by exercising the mind on a continual basis. Solving crosswords, Sudoku or puzzles are effective in training the mind, increasing concentration and boosting creative self-expression. The focus should, however, be on the process rather than the final product. Just as players, singers and athletes maintain and enhance their ability through continual practice, our brains also benefit from regular exercise. It draws its nutrition from imaginative and experiential narrations and writings.

7. Experiment and reflect

Experiment with content and processes on a continual basis during your teaching, and reflect on them to bring further refinement. Renew teaching methods and techniques as often as possible to keep it fresh and interesting for students. In this way you will also save yourself from any possibility of burnout. A teacher enjoys teaching and students enjoy learning when a teacher weaves into his teaching the elements of surprise, fun and humour. Students are fond of those teachers who show patience, tolerance and are ready to explain till it is clear to them. Involve learners in participatory, creative, and open-ended quizzes and games, and productive and investigatory activities to give them the thrill of discovery and success.

Conclusion

Thus, in the present-day context, creativity and readiness for change have vital significance for the children. In the futuristic perspective, they would require an adaptive, integrative outlook in facing problems and conditions for which there are no set patterns or precedents. At this stage, it can be argued that teachers with a general understanding of creative behaviour and equipped with creative teaching skills will be able to provide opportunities for every child to learn creatively, grow creatively and live life creatively. As a matter of fact just imparting information, developing skills or mere certification is not the aim of education, rather it should strive to develop a trained intellect ready to suitably adjust in the fast changing world.

4
Science, Humanity and Spirituality

The motive power of India's forward march throughout the ages has been *sarvabhutahite rata*—universal well-being, *nirbairah sarvabhuteshu*—without enmity towards any entity and *ekata*—unity. It always believed in keeping peace and harmony with nature and its elements: air, water, earth, herbs, forest and animals, sun and moon, planets and stars. But during the last two hundred or so years, the process of industrialisation and resulting technological choices have led to an economic polarisation of the world into the affluent haves and the poor have-nots. These inequalities exist even today between countries. Ever expanding consumption is putting severe stress on the environment. Therefore, the need of the hour is a commitment towards the welfare of humanity, based on human values, scientific temper and rational outlook.

Rational science advocates the pursuit of knowledge through senses and reasoning. It explores, experiments and infers from observational data obtained through the senses. Conclusions are then drawn based on their rational analysis. Scientific knowledge thus created is utilised by the outside world for enhancing material comforts, improving efficiency in doing things and ensuring security from outside interference. It is well known that scientific truths, thus arrived at, have often been negated or modified in the face of further evidence. Hence, the knowledge deduced from sense experience is always contingent and probable. Also, sense perceptions may even be distorted since observations are always subjective. In the mad race for power and comfort, we often overlook the limitations of science.

Science as a modern discipline explores the natural environment, extends its investigations to the outer world and beyond for adding to the material wealth. It provides further means of comfort and empowers ambitious minds for further hegemony and control. One can hardly deny the fact that scientific inquiry, scientific temper and the quest for prosperity and better living are laudable and important objectives in the modern world. Science, to that extent, is an interesting discipline. Learning of science becomes meaningful only when we apply rational thinking in whatever we do or say, display a readiness to critically analyse things and happenings, believe in doing and experimenting and are ready to revise in the face of new evidence. Scientists are always open to new ideas. With the progressive refinement of technological tools, science becomes more exact, thus ensuring that it reaches as close to truth as possible. No one can deny the fact that it is modern science that alone can solve the problems of hunger, poverty and conditions of insanitation, and illiteracy. It can remove many social evils such as superstition and deadening of harmful customs and traditions. Science helps explore and utilise vast resources and stops waste by recycling and reusing.

Proverbially, science has virtually conquered the planet. It has explored the moon and has overcome the natural limits of travel and communication. It stands at the dawn of a new era, ready to move further into space and perhaps inhabit other planets. With the help of science, we can control our environment, markedly reduce diseases and extend our lifespan. The most vital and hopeful of the changes that it has brought about in human behaviour have been the development of scientific outlook and scientific approach to solving problems. Einstein with his rare foresight had commented long ago that the unleashed power of atom is bound to change everything. And now, we find ourselves in a situation that requires the evolution of a common humanity founded on a comprehensive view of man (*Vasudhaiva Kutumbakam*), which alone can guarantee the survival of mankind.

Science and Human Values

During ancient times science, spiritualism and ethics in India were intertwined. The Dalai Lama writes, "Unfortunately, we may easily fall into the trap of thinking that the keys to happiness are material well being on the one hand and the power conferred by knowledge on the other". The ultimate objective is striking a balance between inward tranquillity and outward madness, mental peace, and physical comfort and between science and spirituality. Science has brought mighty changes in every field of life. But not all of them have been for the good of humanity. Exclusive emphasis on science and technology has been able to produce only a materialistic civilisation. The prevailing consumer culture ignores the higher values of mankind. It has led to a crisis wherein humanity is faced with the threat of nuclear war, exhaustion of earth's natural resources, imbalance in the eco-system, environmental pollution and widespread environmental as well as moral degeneration. Jawaharlal Nehru declared at the 1947 Science Congress that the vital role of science in India is to fight ignorance, poverty and disease, and function as a powerful instrument to bring about a social transformation so that millions could live longer and happier lives. He said humanity cannot live on reactors alone. The great path of science is to be tempered by something and that something is spirituality. Indeed, if the world is not to destroy itself, there is a need for human values for survival and at the same time a need for a scientific temper and rational outlook.

Limitations of Rational—Logical Approach

The present-day rational scientific approach alone may not be able to solve many mysteries of nature. One must realise the limitations of the rational–logical approach. Search for true knowledge may require scientists to transcend logic to ensure complete happiness—external happiness and internal happiness, leading to physical, mental as well as spiritual satisfaction of human beings. Hence, the present-day scientific culture may be termed as lopsided because it leads humanity to complete materialism with a total neglect of life values like tolerance, unity in diversity, peaceful living, the divinity of mankind and respect for all forms of life. This has resulted in the culture of violence, creating fear through terror and distrust among fellow human beings. The answer may lie in the synthesis of the two aspects of human life, namely material and spiritual. Erwin Schrodinger maintains, "Our science – Greek Science – is based on objectification, ...But I do believe that this is precisely the point where our present way of thinking does need to be amended, perhaps by a bit of blood-transfusion from Eastern thought".

Science and Transempirical Realities

We find that, on the one hand, science is an ongoing quest for the knowledge of reality as much as it is accessible to reason and experience. On the other hand, it cannot inquire into the transempirical realities. Science as such, therefore, has always been honest enough to be silent about the spiritual realm, which is beyond its scope. Hence, the rejection of transempirical reality on the basis of scientific knowledge based on empiricism is itself an unscientific attitude. Denial of the supernatural and the non-empirical realm of reality on the basis of our partial knowledge of natural empirical world has no justification either in science or in human experience.

Within a human being, both spiritual and temporal have to be perfectly harmonised. Gandhiji advocated for a balanced development of an individual, i.e., his physical , intellectual and spiritual development must go hand in hand. Purely intellectual or heavily material culture bears in its heart the seeds of death. Arnold Toynbee predicted, "It is already becoming clear that a chapter of world history which had a Western beginning will have to have an Indian ending if it is not to end in the self-destruction of the human race".

In spite of all the scientific and technological advancements resulting in vast materialistic achievements, man is hardly able to rest upon secure foundations. As the world shrinks and becomes 'one world' or a 'global village' through technological unification, the forces that make for destruction are intensified. In spite of all-pervading rational outlook, it is hard to ignore that there is something beyond the scientific positive knowledge.

The ideal of world peace can be realised only if modern scientific thought admits the fact that the universe has a divine origin, and that man has a transempirical dimension as well. Swami Vivekananda firmly believed that India could be saved only by preserving its spirituality and cultural heritage.

Make Man the Focus of Science

The very survival of mankind depends on creating a new kind of social institution and tradition, without which the new knowledge of science would bring the ultimate disaster. It is by continuously striving to make Man the focus of science that we imbue it with a sense of values, without which science may act as a destroyer of mankind instead of being a liberator. The way Albert Einstein put it, "a passionate sense of social justice and social responsibility would tell us that statements of scientific facts and relations cannot produce ethical directions which are so badly needed for the world today".

Scientists and technologists, particularly in developing countries, need to seriously deliberate upon the vision of a true scientific society portrayed by Acharya Vinoba Bhave. In his view, "a true scientific society will be one where men will build houses of one storey rather than ten and see that each house has open space around it so that light and air can enter. Science will improve health so much that medicines will scarcely be needed, though the very best remedies will be available if need should arise. There will be doctors, but their services will not be much in demand. Good spectacles will be available, but men of scientific outlook will take care of their eyesight. In the same way, aeroplanes will continue to fly, but they will be needed only occasionally; men will prefer to walk, and in a scientific world, there will be little need of artificial lighting, for people will prefer to spend the night sleeping under the stars. Science will not be used to deprive man of healthful bodily labour, but to lighten his burdens and to increase his vitality and vigour".

The fact of life is that the exclusive emphasis upon science and technology today has been able to produce only a materialistic civilisation and consumer culture in which the higher values of mankind are ignored. It has led to the present crisis of humanity.

Pollution of air, water and land has become a universal problem. Diseases associated with urban living have increased. Noise and congestion are adding to physical and mental distress. The reliance of modern technology upon the combustion of fossil fuels has caused a rise in atmospheric carbon dioxide. There is a major increase in the amount of waste products. Unfortunately, the facilities for their scientific disposal are grossly inadequate. The land upon which humans depend for their food has been seriously impaired. Well-meaning scientists have to change these trends to save humanity.

Human's concern for a peaceful life and harmonious coexistence with their fellow beings seem to have been never so explicit as in the modern age. The International Commission on Education in its report Learning the Treasure Within, talks about one of the pillars of education in this millennium as 'learning to live together'. To deprive humans of their essential transcendental dimension, which finds its expression in their religious and spiritual experiences, is to reduce them to something less than what they really are.

Although many thinkers attach great importance to the achievements of science and technology, they totally disregard the genuine religious and spiritual experiences of saints and seers. The scientific community refuses to take into account the supernatural and extra-empirical facts of reality in its interpretation of humans and the world. Obviously, a partial view of existence based upon the rational and empirical findings of science can yield only a distorted picture of human reality. A philosophy which does not take into account all the facts of experience whether physical, psychological or spiritual, will always be proved inadequate to lead mankind to a life of happiness and peaceful existence.

Science and Humanity

Further, organised religion is found to be a challenge to the idea of world community. War and global terrorism have marred the modern world more than ever before. Humanity is perhaps living through the most dangerous period in all its history. A deep feeling of insecurity has gripped us all. Humans must and will always have some form of religion because to live without faith is impossible. It is an irony that although we are aware of the emptiness of our life, we are not able to find a way out of it. The dogmas of traditional religions cannot solve our problems anymore. This is because they have neglected the deeper humane element. The cause of present-day tension is the lack of adjustment between science and humanity. Science has to be coordinated with the spirit of humanism and that is the most urgent need of mankind today.

In this world of science and technology, one confronts with the artificial environment, observes the sophisticated manipulation of machines and techniques, but alas the human element is gradually being eliminated. We may recall that in the mediaeval period the world was considered a sacred order established by God. Every natural resource in the form of plant, birds, or animal, the sun, moon and stars, the water bodies and the mountains all were seen as God's creation. Consequently, these were considered sacred. A great deal of effort in the mediaeval world went into preserving, fostering and nourishing this sense. The highest type of activity was that of contemplation. But intoxicated by scientific power and technological superiority, we have destroyed this type of world.

Our society is man-made, not a divine order. It represents a projection of the human mind that has cut its links with the divine. Its ideals are purely temporal and finite and concern only the material welfare of its members. In this artificial world, one can exist on the condition that they adopt, adapt and adjust to its needs and requirements. This human-made world demands its inhabitant to be just a cog in the machine, which is basically impersonal and not human, has no heart, no feelings, no emotions and no spontaneity.

Fortunately, scientists themselves now admit that the best of their theories are but hypotheses. They are aware that these, far from being reached inductively on the basis of objective data, are for the most part simply postulated as the most probable explanation or interpretation of certain data. Also, this again is done in accordance with a particular model, which the scientist in question happens to have accepted. Basically, scientific theories, hypotheses, explanation or scientific truths are statements which either can be verified with reference to empirical evidence or experiment or at least cannot be shown to be false with reference to such evidence or experiment.

If our society is to recover its health, science and humanism must converge by declaring the welfare of mankind as its central theme. Similarly, we must get away from a religion that does not have respect for the dignity and the rights of human beings. A religion which has lost the power of creative expression in conformity with the needs and demands of our age should have no place in the society. No religion can hope to survive if it does not satisfy the scientific temper and foster the unity of the world. What is needed today is the preservation of the precious substance of religious reality by translating it in terms and needs of our own day. As a matter of fact, there should be only one religion in the world and that should be the religion of humanity.

Need for a Holistic Approach

A complete reversal of direction is necessary to conceptualise a new concept of science that is holistic in approach towards mankind and transcends the sphere of the rational. Let me end with the sayings of Lev Tolstoy, "The highest wisdom is one. The highest wisdom knows but one science – the science of the whole, the science that explains the whole creation and the place of man in it".

Keeping in view the inhuman social realities of present-day society, it may be concluded that the scientific intelligentsia should come together and review the science curriculum based on a balanced and holistic approach in the search for the ultimate truth and meaning of life. Education in science and technology should transform itself into a complete philosophy of life, capable of bringing about genuine happiness and universal peace and harmony through recognition of the material, rational as well as spiritual and transcendental dimensions of reality.

The science of inner self, sometimes termed inner engineering, insists on the development of faculties of intuition, insight and wisdom. Spiritual science crosses the borders of sense knowledge. It crosses the borders of intellectual knowledge. Instead it believes in growing inward, discovering the inner self and inner unity through inner vision and intuition. Hence, reducing humans to the level of what the reason can perceive or understand about them is to dehumanise them.

Such a science gets restricted to the outer world only. We should critically examine and determine the characteristics and limitations of the scientific reasoning because knowledge of science and technology is primarily based on rational analysis. This reasoning is limited to the material and the conceptions. Humans and their world cannot be fully appreciated within the limited sphere of reasoning, experimentation and observation. For the engineering of the inner world, one has to take recourse to contemplation, meditation and intuition.

5
Education for Women's Equality

Education is one of the most important tools for achieving social justice and equality for women. Educational development of girls works as a potent liberating force for half of the nation's population. It is crucial not only in elevating their status but also for accelerating economic development and social transformation. The National Education Policy 2020 "recognises the special and critical role that women play in society and in shaping social mores–not only in their own generation but in the next one; therefore, providing a quality education to girls is the best way to increase the education levels for these Socio-Economically Disadvantaged Groups (SEDGs) not just in the present but also in future generations". Incidentally, 'education for women' also was one of the important thrust areas in the National Policy on Education (NPE), 1986.

Education for women in the country suffers from both quantitative as well as qualitative shortcomings, especially in rural areas. When we consider education for women, it includes education for girls in general and in vocational or professional fields. Statistics show that girls comprise the major chunk of the non-enrolled and dropout child population in the age group of 6–14 years.

Similar dismal situation is noticed in the area of vocational education for girls. Their participation in vocational education is low. The range of vocational courses generally offered to them is relatively limited. A traditional gender bias dominates the vocational field too. Access of girls to many non-traditional vocational courses is restricted in a very subtle manner. Although there are sporadic examples of girls breaking the shackles, but the tradition bound society does not generally offer these courses to girls. Girls, too, are found reluctant to opt for them due to ignorance or lack of encouragement. Studies show that most of the co-education or only girls institutions deliberately follow a restrictive policy in allocating vocational courses to girls.

An unbiased analysis of the situation will lead us to the question of specific needs, interests and aptitudes of the boys and girls on the one hand and requirements of the society and industry on the other. We cannot deny the fact that boys and girls differ from each other not only in their physical appearance but also in their thinking, temperament and physical as well as intellectual abilities. There are certain personality traits which are more pronounced in boys than girls and vice-versa. A close look at their biological, intellectual and personality traits will indicate that boys and girls, or *purush and prakriti,* have been conceived by nature as complementary to each other. Each is incomplete without the other.

If *purush* has been identified with *pourush* or *parakram,* the *prakriti* has been conceived of as mother earth or *Shakti.* Both have their specific roles to play in life and society. Therefore, all facilities should be equally provided to both at home and school to help them actualise their inherent potentialities, which are at times markedly different. Here comes the role of education. One must remember that the objective of education is not to iron out these specificities from their personalities and mould them into replicas of each other. The aim is to provide an environment conducive for unfolding of the unique talents by both boys and girls.

There are many aspects of life, especially the finer ones, in which girls can excel given the opportunity. Experience shows that in jobs requiring endurance, sensitivity, compassion, understanding of human nature and realities, accurate and critical judgment, the freshness of views, calculated and cool handling of certain types of situations, aesthetically appealing and practical solutions, better human relations, deciding of strategies especially in adversities are aptly handled by the female. If opportunities are made available to girls for training them in such intellectual and vocational pursuits which bring in the interplay of the above personality factors, the education system can produce an independent workforce, which instead of jamming the same frequency as those of boys, will carve out a frequency band of its own, which will allow them to utilise their inherent capabilities to be much more efficacious. In addition, it will ensure better efficiency and quality in these types of jobs.

It is generally observed that only soft options or the so-called 'feminine' courses are earmarked for girls. Another disturbing trend being perpetuated is that, as a rule, only those courses are considered 'suitable' for women that fall within the purview of home science. Curiously enough although the best chefs and dressmakers the world over happen to be males, boys are neither offered nor opt for home science courses in schools. Unfortunately, this deeply enshrined 'home science syndrome' virtually cuts off all other options for girls/women. At the same time, instances are also not rare to find women preferring, whatever may be the reason, only the time-tested traditional vocational courses such as tailoring, knitting and embroidery, cooking, secretarial practice, teaching and training and research and development, even if nontraditional courses particularly from the areas of engineering, agriculture or para-medical are made open to them. This preference for home or office-based courses prevail among girls probably due to the conservative outlook of parents, shortage of trained women teachers and other socio–cultural realities like time to be devoted, working conditions and place of work.

In order to promote women's participation in nontraditional occupations, as well as in existing and emergent technologies, they would require easy access to modern occupational information, vocational guidance services specially designed for women and diversified training facilities. There is an urgent need to neutralise the accumulated distortions of the past and move forward by positive interventions like redesigned curricula, textbooks, training and orientation of more women teachers and sensitisation of decision-makers and administrators to foster the development of new values.

Courses such as audio-visual technology, ophthalmic technology, photography, textile printing, accountancy and taxation, interior decoration, food preservation and processing, dietician, nursing, teaching, management, administration and a host of other vocations do not require strenuous physical work. Finger dexterity, understanding of the application processes and a rational insight into the practical subject matter are the main requirements for success in these. In addition to these wage employment-oriented vocational courses, women can be offered many self-employment courses as well. The latter would not only challenge the entrepreneurial abilities among them but would also be useful to women in rural areas where opportunities for wage employment are limited. Self-help groups have recently been doing well in rural areas. These need to be supported and extended further.

Often after marriage women are not in a position to take up full-time vocations outside their homes. However, they may be willing to take up some form of productive work at home to attain total or partial economic independence or even to supplement their family income. Part-time or online self-employment of this nature will surely have a positive bearing on the self-confidence and social status of women. Recently this trend of online self-employment in women has markedly increased during and after the COVID-19 pandemic to obviate the acute financial problems faced due to migration and layoffs.

Thus, job opportunities in the context of women's employment may be seen from three angles. The first relates to wage employment opportunities in the production, distribution and service sectors; the second to self-employment as an individual entrepreneur or through a group project and the third to home-based part-time or online self-employment. Hence, entrepreneurship development programmes in diverse areas should form an integral part of the curriculum of all vocational courses for women.

Efforts will also have to be made simultaneously to create a climate conducive to encourage more girls and women to take up new fields. They should be motivated to come forward and join vocational courses spread over a variety of areas.

Establishment of model vocational schools for women in select districts in every state would ensure enrolment in good measure. These schools having residential facilities and well-equipped laboratories, workshop and libraries should be run exclusively for women.

It will be desirable to establish vocational centres with comprehensive offering in the vicinity of industries and advanced training institutions. If need be, provision should also be made for incentives in the form of stipends or scholarship. In order to encourage self-employment these centres should have special cells offering consultancy services, and technical and financial assistance to the needy women.

Multiple strategies will have to be adopted. These would include motivational campaigns, consultancy services, establishment of special institutions, development of entrepreneurship and support for self-employment. In addition to formal courses leading to self- and wage employment, non-formal vocational courses specifically tailor made for women will go a long way in elevating their status and making them equal partners in the overall economic development of the country.

But this is possible only when a girl is taken as an independent or individual personality with its specific needs, and not always placed as an opponent of a boy or an equivalent. Educationists concerned with women's education should search for a viable educational and vocational model for girls which neither simply apes the West nor dogmatically sticks to traditional concept of *abla nari.* This will require a thorough analysis of the contemporary Indian society, vital security needs of women and economic independence coupled with the present-day social and economic values, beliefs and constraints.

Such a need-based and culturally oriented educational model will not be based on a 'confrontation model'. Instead, it will be a combination of a 'complementary or supplementary model' and a 'self-reliant, one based on self-respect, creativity and dignity. In the spectrum of this model, there will be invisible threads of cohesion between man and woman, at the same time retaining distinct bands of self-reliance and respectable personalities. This model of women's education must provide for the full flowering of their unique talents and personal qualities.

While there is no denying of the fact that education for women is of paramount importance for a progressive society, it is the working out of the Indian model, having its roots in Indian socio-economic culture, which requires to be seriously debated upon. As in many other fields, this area of education has also been dominated by disgruntled elements echoing the western style of women's liberation, mainly based on freedom from tradition and culture. In recent years, there has been a spurt in women's organisations and women's forums particularly in the country's urban belt. Their declared policy is to voice the 'deplorable' plight of women in society and to fight for equal rights in all walks of life and work. Apparently, there is nothing wrong in these ideals. But distortion takes place when, driven by ulterior motives, these are applied to education and employment without taking into consideration the social, economic, cultural and traditional realities of our society.

It is often argued that since boys and girls are equal in the eyes of law, no subjects in the school curriculum should be earmarked for girls alone. Instead, every effort should be made to wean them away from traditional subjects like home science and embroidery. They should be encouraged to go in for those courses which are generally opted by boys, like engineering, driving, security services or commerce and business. The goal of the enthusiasts is that no subject or job should be the sole prerogative of boys and that girls must penetrate all the citadels of men. This has resulted in an unhealthy competition between men and women for the same jobs. It has been observed that it is ultimately the girls who suffer the most due to this trend.

Often men grumble that while a boy getting a job means bread for a whole family, a woman spends her pay packet on cosmetics, luxury items or entertainment. Women on the other hand profess that they do not want to beg from men for petty items of their own requirements. While there may be some element of truth in the allegations of both, the point to ponder is what is the real concept of equality? Does equality mean that both boys and girls should be given ample opportunities in education and training at all stages, or does it mean that boys and girls in exactly equal numbers should jostle for jobs with each other or aim to capture the same seats or positions?

In order to come to a reasonable conclusion, we probably require an impartial view. The main contention here is to ensure independence, equality, dignity, livelihood and avenues for talent expression for women. This is possible without confrontation with boys because such confrontation many a times breeds hatred and bitterness between men and women, which is detrimental for both. Rather it should be a cooperative, complementary and supportive effort to enable women to stand on their own and lead a creatively satisfying life. With a view to availing equal opportunity, boys and girls should have an undifferentiated curriculum at all levels. The system has to inclusive so that there is no gender stereotyping, either in general education or vocational education.

Conclusion

In Indian society, husband and wife have been termed as the two wheels of a cart. In this analogy, no wheel of the cart vies with the other to go faster, nor do they cross each other's way. They move freely on their own paths keeping pace with each other and taking the cart forward in a rhythmic movement to its destination. The attainment of this rhythmic combination of man and woman in life should be the aim of education. This will, of course, not exclude boys who should also be positively educated regarding the contributions that women can make to society, their needs, interests, abilities and special qualities. Boys need to understand and positively appreciate a girl's personality better, thereby instilling in them respect for women and to ensure specific identity of both in the society.

Teachers at every level have to be duly sensitised through in-service and pre-service teacher training programmes regarding specific aptitudes of boys and girls. A balanced view towards gender equality and dignity of girls must prevail in every educational institution. Both boys and girls should be given appropriate opportunities and educational/vocational inputs in addition to the core curriculum so that they feel free to optimise the flowering of their specific talents and innate capabilities. The National Education Policy has rightly directed that "Teachers will aim to encourage students with singular interests and/ or talents in the classroom by giving them supplementary enrichment material and guidance and encouragement and will help them to organise such Topic-centred Clubs and Circles through specific funding allocated for this purpose, and will recommend them to appropriate summer programmes". GOI, MHRD. National Education Policy 2020,4.41, page 18. New Delhi.

In the contemporary Indian society, parents (particularly belonging to middle class) of a girl child do everything possible to convince her that she is not inferior to a boy in any way and has every right to mould herself like a boy in every field. She is brought up and dressed like a boy, addressed as '*beta*', encouraged to play boy's games, choose same courses or specialisations as boys and compete for jobs that hitherto have been the citadels of boys. In other words, she is not allowed to excel herself as a girl. Perforce she is taught martial arts of various types to fight boys in the name of self-defence. This confrontational mindset has led to broken homes and shameful domestic violence and criminal conspiracies. Such discords and gender enmity can be prevented if equality is perceived as equal opportunity, optimum flowering of respective unique talents and respect and dignity of each other's divine personalities. They need to be recognised as boys and girls and allowed to excel in any field of their choice in line with their aptitude and inclination. Education must try to bridge this divide by positive interventions and better counselling.

6

Violence in Drawing Room

COVID-19 pandemic brought along with it a new way of living under total or partial 'lockdown' for an extended period. During this period, many old practices like visiting friends and families, gossiping in groups, roaming or window shopping in malls took a back seat, whereas new cultural practices like staying within the four walls, working from home, use of telemedicine, online shopping and e-business emerged in a big way almost universally. Lockdown restrictions have indirectly given a big boost to electronic media. Digital literacy has taken the front seat. However, continuous staying at home together with other family members. Both young and old. Did bring in feelings of closeness and togetherness. Unfortunately, at the same time it also resulted in some unhealthy social practices like rise in domestic violence, more and more use of smartphones and viewing of TV for long hours.

Living in close proximity all the time often brought to surface the differences of opinion, clash of interest and accompanying mental stress. Fortunately, one important element that helped in reducing violent expression of differences and unwanted conversations has been the use of virtual media by young and old alike. It is observed that members of the family, to remain away from controversy and clash of interest, kept themselves busy in smartphone and/or viewing of television. These two versatile gadgets, kept people at a distance or made them to remain aloof even though physically they were compelled to stay together.

Historically, television first entered our drawing rooms with educative and entertaining content in programmes like Chitrhaar, Bharat Darshan, Krishi Darshan, Yoga and News & Views. Gradually humorous serial episodes, family dramas and serials showing complexities of social relationships entered the small screen, which was welcomed wholeheartedly by people in general and housewives in particular. Epics like Ramayana and Mahabharata broke all records of viewing. Television viewing remained soothing and soft and hence, popular among families.

Television being the main source of entertainment, information and news, people often fail to appreciate that TV has a powerful influence on its viewers. It not only shapes the behaviour of people especially children but also goes to develop their value systems through its content, presentation and variety. Television can be gainfully used in developing positive value systems and shaping socially desirable, progressive and patriotic sensitivities.

But with the introduction and promotion of unethical and undesirable viewing content by different interest groups, the two versatile media—the smartphone and the small screen—practically have become a nuisance and breeding ground of violent and criminal tendencies among children, adolescents and adults alike. These include movies, web series and episodes depicting excessive violence, violent online video games, use of filthy and double meaning conversations and scenes, crime reporting in the garb of true stories and introducing serials like Savdhaan India, Mauka-e-vardaat, Crime Patrol, and so on. These programmes on both TV and smartphone are full of violent and sadistic content totally unsuitable for viewing in drawing rooms within a family set up. Exposure to such domestically offensive episodes and online content increases the risk of children and adults behaving aggressively. Noise, violent and inhuman contents affect the mental and emotional health adversely.

Violence among youth is a growing concern in modern society. While there are many causes for violent behaviour, research has shown that television does play a role in promoting violent behaviour, particularly in younger children. The entertainment industry implicitly recognises this fact. With the help of a rating system, it recommends certain programmes not to be watched by children of a certain age. Yet, the number of violent acts on television has not abated and children watch TV extensively for long hours. There is much research evidence to indicate that violence shown in media contribute to aggressive behaviour. They even cause desensitisation to violence in men.

Viewers who see such content for a long time are less likely to help others, feel sympathetic toward victims and express empathy. This is borne by the fact that often we come across news items about accident victims who lie bleeding and writhing in pain, but people make videos rather than helping them. It has also been found that youth who view media violence on a regular basis is more likely to exhibit antisocial behaviour. Such behaviours range from imitative violent behaviour to criminal violence and an increased feelings of hostility.

Television today has reached every home. There will be very few people who do not watch one or the other programme on the TV. Also, being confined to an apartment, one has to witness many other programmes being watched by others. TV being a home appliance with a strong appeal, it must follow some social and family norms. It should not compete with the big screen. I would say that television should even have its own cadre of anchors and actors. It should have its own research wing. TV serials or programmes must stop copying from films and shun violence, sadness, crime and the use of filthy language. It must always keep in mind the home environment and the likely influence it may have on innocent viewers. Viewing of movies in cinema halls and multiplexes is always at the discretion of the viewer but a similar degree of discretion is absent in the case of television because of collective viewing by a family most of the time. The most vulnerable groups are children and adolescents.

Unfortunately, all channels do not show programmes that are suitable to be beamed in every drawing room. Relationships, facts and figures, statistics, violence, revenge, love, hatred, crime, etc., whatever is shown on TV, most people, particularly youngsters, consider them to be the norm or standard to be followed. This is because children derive their values, attitudes and beliefs from whatever happens in the presence of their elders within the home, including those viewed on TV.

Home is the first social agency for socialisation. Children's behaviour is largely governed by the ethos, environment, emotions and conflicts they experience at home. But much of today's television programming is violent, TRP driven or presented with some motives. Alas! You do not have a single news channel where one can get the day's news in a neutral fashion, presented in a coherent, clear, sophisticated and civilised way. All news channels today are increasing noise pollution within the home. Often, they go much beyond their mandate. They show free-for-all sessions, investigative probes or bullet train version of news, which are at times beyond comprehension. News channels today broadcast everything except standard news in standard language. They lack clarity, coherence, comprehensiveness and lucid presentation.

It is difficult to understand why a family consisting of parents, grandparents and children should be compelled to view episodes which are nothing but pure violence, full of perversion and revenge or hatred. A family instead requires something educative, soothing and informative. Soap operas or serials dedicated to healthy humour, aesthetic scenes and events, social relationships and nourishing content for health, hygiene, spiritual exaltation, emotional intelligence, positive social norms and entrepreneurship refresh the viewers and recreate a hopeful world for people in general.

It is time that a sensor board is created for TV viewing to filter out such content which breeds hatred, violence, sadistic emotions and revengeful attitudes. It should not be left to market forces alone. A national debate needs to be started immediately on the content, number of channels, hours of broadcast, code of conduct for quality and number of advertisements and similar other issues so essential to transform this media into a pleasing experience for families. The content of the advertisements needs to be censored to do away with advertisements of pan-masala, hard drinks, fast food and such others. Scenes of smoking and consuming alcohol give a very wrong message to youngsters.

Also, allowing children to advertise below a certain age should be brought within child labour law.

At the end, it may be argued that there is ample scope to modify the content of programmes by the TV and smartphone providers in order to faithfully discharge their social and moral responsibilities towards the civilised society. Self-introspection, self-evaluation, self-regulation and self-control by these media cannot be overemphasised. In a democracy, media has a vital role to play in evolving a humane, compassionate, peace-loving citizenry to take the civilised society on the path of sustainability and enlightened modernity.

Section 2

Teacher and Teacher Education

7

Students' Perception of a Good Teacher

Society, and especially the Indian society, expects the teacher to be an embodiment of values. Seshadri (1992) maintains that "The teacher should be a person of unimpeachable character and a paragon of virtue". Further, he is expected to inspire children by setting his own example in whatever he says or does. According to the constructivist paradigm, a teacher not only educates the child but simultaneously learns from them in the process. This is because in a participatory teaching-learning set up. learning is mutual in character. It demands patience, consideration and affection. Teaching as a process in no way means conditioning of the child's mind to function as a cog in the social machine. On the contrary, a teacher helps the child to grow into an integrated personality and as a creative human being who is empowered to examine and understand the social norms. Even at times the child should be able to question these norms if a situation so demands.

According to Altekar (1948), the teacher has to be patient and treat his pupils impartially. They are expected to be a person of high character, well grounded in their own branch of knowledge and fluent in delivery. A good teacher has readiness of wit, stock of interesting anecdotes and is capable of instructing and inspiring. Adaval (1979) describes the teacher as one who is tender-hearted, abode of virtue, man or woman of right conduct, respectful to others, humble, speaker of truth and dutiful. They do not utter harsh words and is self-disciplined. In the medieval period, saints like Kabir, Dadu and others described the teacher as one who dispels ignorance and is kind and impartial. Good handwriting and clear and accurate pronunciation are considered essential for a good teacher.

Many educational practitioners and researchers view the practical and relevant routines of day-to-day teaching as equally or more important than the theoretical or philosophical aspects of education (Ralph, 1994b). Many educational administrators view effective teaching as a complex process of reflective practice whereby the professional teacher plans, prepares and orchestrates in a sensible and sensitive fashion a variety of methods, materials and motivating experiences meeting students' learning needs (Darling, Hammond & Sclan, 1992; Eby, 1992; Ralph, 1994a).

Good and effective teachers competently select and utilise a variety of fundamental skills of generic teaching. A meta-analysis of research findings came up with a core group of essential skills. These skills, which include both personal and professional attributes comprise communication skills, planning skills, presentation abilities—clear explanations, posing clear and concise questions, evaluating pupil's work and applying varied instructional methods and media. In one of the earliest and most comprehensive studies reported in 1934 probed into the question, 'What do pupils like and dislike in their teacher?' The study identified the following ten characteristics based on a survey of 3,725 high school seniors:

1. Is helpful with schoolwork
2. Explains lessons and assignments clearly and thoroughly and uses examples in teaching
3. Cheerful, happy, good-natured, jolly, has a sense of humour and can take a joke
4. Human, friendly, companionable and 'one of us'
5. Interested in and understands pupils
6. Makes work interesting, creates a desire to work, makes class work a pleasure
7. Strict, has control of the class and commands respect
8. Impartial, shows no favouritism, has no 'pets'

9. Not cross, crabby, grouchy, nagging or sarcastic
10. A pleasing personality.

Alexander (1960) has outlined the characteristics of good teachers as follows:

1. Personal Equipment

- Concern for the individual
- Emotional stability
- Enthusiasm
- Intelligence
- Integrity
- Knowledge
- Personal charm
- Skill in communication

2. Ways of Teaching

- Effective relations with individual pupils
- Adequate planning and preparation
- Wise use of teaching aids
- Involvement of pupils in varied learning experiences
- Active leadership of the learning group

3. Professional Behaviour

- Helping other teachers in general school
- Cooperating in taking responsibilities
- Cooperating in educational improvement
- Strengthening professional organisations
- Maintaining ethical relations with the school administration and the pupils

In India, Menon (1949) mentioned the following qualities in a 'good teaching personality':

- Ability to maintain discipline
- Teaching skill
- Intelligence

- Fairness
- Cooperation

Adaval (1979) collected opinions from 34 experts on an open-ended questionnaire about the qualities of a successful teacher. These were grouped under:

- Friendliness, cheerfulness, sense of Humour
- Honesty, impartiality, fairness
- Love for children, affectionate
- Sympathetic intuition, sympathy and understanding
- Character, moral integrity, uprightness
- Presence of physical qualities, appearance, impressiveness
- Sociability, extroversion
- Love, loyalty, idealism for the profession
- Patience
- Sincerity, earnestness

Menon (1949) concluded that "the data available now shows that experts and pupils agree on all vital matters regarding good and bad teachers". He also opines that "the results prove clearly that pupils' opinions are clear and definite and that these can't be ignored. Their opinion should be given proper weightage".

Gupta (1979) concluded in his study that the most frequently mentioned factors helpful in classroom teaching were:

- The blackboard work
- Correcting oral mistakes
- Explaining difficult points
- General knowledge
- Handwriting
- Knowledge of the subject
- Maintaining discipline
- Power of oral expression
- Revision of main points

- Skill in questioning
- Use of material aids

The research findings discussed previously provide useful indicators regarding the qualities of a good and effective teacher.

Investigation by the Author

The author himself made an attempt to collect opinions from a cross-section of pupils cutting across grades VI to XII, who were interviewed regarding their views on the 'qualities of a good teacher'. The basic premise for the present investigation was that it is the pupils who are in direct contact with the teacher. Therefore, in all probability, it is the pupils who can be considered to be the most competent and better judges to enumerate the qualities of a good teacher. They, therefore, were given the opportunity to offer their first-hand opinions based on their personal experiences.

The pupils in the sample were drawn from the demonstration school, Regional Institute of Education, Bhopal. The total sample consisting of 333 students (both boys and girls) were asked to respond freely to an open-ended question viz. 'In your opinion, what should be the qualities of a good teacher?'

After careful analysis of the responses received and collating them into broad but distinct categories, it was interesting to note that most of these categories of responses were related to the personal qualities of the teachers. The pupils were thus found to be highly concerned about the teacher as an individual and their behaviour which they exhibited during numerous interactions with pupils both within and outside the classroom. However, there were few categories which focused on the professional qualities possessed by the teachers as well.

(i) Personal Qualities

Some of the personal qualities mentioned by the majority of the sample students were summed up as follows:

1. Understands pupils; appreciates and tries to solve educational and personal problems; respects their feelings and emotions; frank, friendly and good rapport with pupils

2. Loving and parent-like behaviour; pleasing manners; good personality; not rude; does not use bad language or terrorise
3. Impartial; equal attention to every child; no discrimination or favour; knows pupils individually
4. Punctual and regular in taking classes; doesn't leave class in-between; starts teaching right from day one
5. Displays personality characteristics like being brave, kind, sympathetic, intelligent, creative, cooperative, polite, tolerant, honest, approachable, confident, patient and showing no anger; does not ridicule or insult any child.
6. In addition to knowledge about subject matter content, inspiring and giving information about good manners, good character, new and latest developments, moral education, good habits and qualities, good books, the right path and good *sanskar*
7. Punishing and scolding only if wrong—neither unnecessarily nor out of proportion
8. Not cruel; neither too strict nor too liberal
9. Helpful in distress or in need; help in solving personal or educational problems
10. Maintains discipline in class.
11. Praises, encourages and inspires children for best performance; shows bravery; plays and participates in activities; allows children to express themselves
12. Asks questions to all frequently, encourages questions from children, readily responds to questions from all students
13. Exhibits good and exemplary conduct, has no bad habits; a role model to students; possesses good moral values
14. Does not punish or scold on minor issues; does not beat, scold, insult or make fun instead gives them chance to mend their ways; values self-respect of students

15. Strict but witty; has a sense of humour; kind; commands respect; discipline enforced through personal influence
16. (a) Dutiful, sincere, dedicated and honest
    (b) Selfless and broadminded
    (c) Calm, good-natured and soft-spoken
17. Special attention to weak students

(ii) Professional Qualities

1. Teaches well with love and dedication, interesting style of teaching, devises new ways of teaching, explains willingly and repeatedly till students understand properly, and uses teaching aids
2. Well qualified, highly educated and experienced.
3. Gives reasonable amount of homework and checks regularly
4. Specialist/master of his own subject

Analysis and Interpretation of Results

Analysis of the pupil's responses in this study indicates spectacular similarity and a consistent line of thinking on the part of the pupils, right from earlier research to the modern ones on the subject. One even notices similar adjectives and active verbs being used by them to describe a good teacher.

A revealing finding having far-reaching implications for teacher education is that the responses mainly focus on the personality of the teachers. Their behaviour towards pupils in and outside the classroom receives major importance. Professional qualities like content specialisation come much below in the rank order. This is probably because teachers in that school were fully qualified to teach the subject content. This finding, however, emphasises on proper selection of pupil-teachers, catching them young and a prolonged training period. Only those with exemplary personal and social qualities should be allowed to enter the profession.

Interestingly in the realm of personal attributes, the highest rank goes to a teacher who treats the students with love and care, tries to understand them both as a person and as students.

Sample students gave utmost weightage to impartiality and good moral character. In their opinion, a good teacher is one who helps them in solving their personal as well as educational problems. A teacher who is always friendly and frank with them, maintains good personal rapport, respects the feelings and emotions of the pupils, and encourages and inspires them receives a higher rank in their preference.

A teacher must be quite conscious and careful while interacting with the students. This is because the present study indicates that pupils closely watch the teacher's behaviour during their interactions within and outside the classroom. The study findings revealed that majority of the sample students (60 %) would like to see their good teacher to have an attractive personality, exhibit loving and parent-like behaviour and display pleasing manners while interacting. A good teacher is neither rude nor a source of terror. The language used during conversation should be soft and civilised.

Each child desires to be attended to by the teacher. Any kind of favouritism, partiality or discrimination by the teacher is not acceptable to them. 49 percent of pupils, therefore, expressed that a good teacher must know every child individually and give equal attention to every child without any discrimination or favour. 47 percent of the sample students value punctuality and regularity the most on the part of the teacher. A good teacher in the opinion of 36 percent pupils is one who displays personality characteristics like being brave, kind, sympathetic, intelligent, creative, cooperative, polite, tolerant, honest, approachable, confident, patient and showing no anger. Students would like to approach the teacher without fear of being ridiculed or insulted.

Pupils look up to a teacher not simply as a subject matter dispenser but also as a source of general knowledge, inspiration and an epitome of good moral character who shows the right path and instils good *sanskaars* among children.

In the opinion of the students, a good teacher should not be cruel or unduly strict. They should neither be too strict nor too liberal. However, they may punish or scold when someone creates nuisance but not unnecessarily or out of proportion. In their opinion, a good teacher praises, encourages and inspires children to give their best performance, asks questions and readily responds to all queries from every student.

As regards professional qualities of a good teacher, there seems to be total unanimity among students. All of them, without exception, opined that such a teacher teaches well with love and dedication. They devise new ways of teaching and also uses appropriate teaching aids to make it interesting and well-illustrated.

Conclusion

Survey of qualities of a good teacher done earlier in the timeline laid much importance on personal characteristics like good moral character, emotional stability, inner discipline, dutifulness, leadership, encouraging attitude and love and affection towards pupils. Emphasis on knowledge of subject matter and on learning is found mainly during the post-vedic and Buddhist period. During the medieval period, the good teacher was supposed to remove ignorance, did not care for physical pleasures, was kind and impartial and removed all doubts of students through their teachings. As for the contemporary society, the emphasis is on acquiring academic and professional qualifications of a desirable standard. Today a teacher is seen in the context of the larger community, its values and culture.

The results of the present investigation indicate that students these days are more concerned about the teacher's personal qualities, their behaviour during interactions, attitude towards pupils and use of interesting and innovative teaching techniques. Subject matter competence of the teacher is reflected only subsequently in their responses. This may also be because classroom teaching today is only one of the many inputs which otherwise are available in the form of guides, solved questions, coaching classes, variety of help books in libraries and guidance from parents or peers. Internet today has come as a versatile resource to them, including online resources. In the examination-oriented school system, the teacher is relegated to the position of an instructor or just a technician who mechanically covers the syllabus irrespective of students' needs, requirements or individual differences. Pupils, therefore, admire a teacher who tries to understand them, values their individuality and attends to their problems, presenting in the process an example to emulate.

Thus, keeping in view the observations made by the students, one may possibly describe the situation as 'the student is very much alive even today, but the teacher is dead'. The most pressing challenge before any teacher education programme today is 'how to rejuvenate this teacher and bring life into the teaching profession?'

References

Adaval, S. B. (1979) *Quality of Teachers*, Allahabad: Amitabh Prakashan.

Alexander, William M. (1960) *Are You a Good Teacher?* New York: Holt, Rinehart and Winston.

Altekar, A. S. (1948) *Education in Ancient India*, Banaras: Nand Kishore & Bros. p. 52.

Darling, Hammond, L. and Sclan, E. (1992) Policy and Supervision. In C. Clickman (Ed.) *Supervision in Transition*. 1992 Yearbook of the Association for Supervision and Curriculum Development.

Gupta, R. P. (1979) A Study of Some Factors Considered to be Helpful in Class Teaching, Ph.D. Education, Lucknow University.

Menon, T. K. N. (1949) Teachers and Educational Reconstruction. *Indian Journal of Psychology,* XXIV, 1–4.

Ralph, E. (1994a) Enhancing the Supervision of Beginning Teachers: A Canadian Initiative–Teaching and Teacher Education, 10 (2) 185–203.

Ralph, E. (1994b) On Assembling the Pieces: What do Retired Educators Tell Us. *Action in Teacher Education*, 16 (2) 62–72.

Sen Gupta, M. (2002) Personal and Professional Values of an Effective Teacher. *Journal of Value Education,* Vol.1, pp. 98-109, New Delhi.

Seshadri, C. (1992) Values and Education:Philosophical Perspectives, *Education in Values a Source Book*.C. Seshadri, M. A. Khader, G. L. Adhya (Ed.), New Delhi: NCERT.

8
Innovative Experiences in an Experimental School

River water due to its continuous flow is always refreshing, whereas stagnant water in a pond stinks. Similarly, educational practices require innovations on a continual basis to bring fresh life in an institutional ethos. However, innovations in education are hard to come by. Implementing innovative ideas into practice at the field level requires imagination, courage, conviction and a fair amount of good communication skill on the part of an educator. Many pedagogical axioms can be assimilated within the school curriculum by adopting some novel practices, which may on the face of it look very simple but have hidden elements of learning, action and motivation.

In a school situation, working leadership of the Principal and their encouragement for innovation is essential to change the mindset of teachers who feel secure within their comfort zone. Often it is said that 'change the Principal and the school will change automatically'. As a matter of fact, the 'Experimental School' referred to in the title experienced this phenomenon.

A Principal who joined the school was highly authoritarian in his approach. His total focus and emphasis were on academic studies. Consequently, co-curricular activities, games and sports, clubs and other literary societies, health and hygiene-related activities receded to the background during his tenure. The school even skipped annual sports day and annual day function in one of the academic sessions. During working days, at any point of time classes were on and there was pin drop silence in the school. So much so that any visitor could not believe that more than one thousand students were enrolled in the school. The Principal being a local person had close links with state officials and taking its advantage, in his own wisdom, he managed to dissociate the school from the Central Board of Secondary Education, to which it was affiliated, and instead got the school affiliated with the State Board. Excessive attention to academic studies obviously resulted in the school getting distinctions in the State Board's examinations. There was 100 percent result in almost every subject. Therefore, the Principal's room got decorated with certificates awarded by the Board to this effect. Home examination results too were above 80 percent in every class.

But surprisingly, all these obvious positive results led to a gradual diminution in the enrolment of students. At the end of the session, one after the other, parents started withdrawing their wards from the school. Parents of the children leaving the school opined that similar results were available in a number of good schools within the city premises under the State Board. Therefore, why should they send their kids to this experimental school, which is 7 kilometers away from the main city centre and approachable only by school bus? Finally, at the end of four years under this Principal, the school had to face a crisis situation due to the total enrolment going down below six hundred and thereby leaving a number of surplus teachers. Consequently, resentment from the staff followed, and as a result, this Principal had to bow out unceremoniously.

The next Principal who joined the school was firm in his commitment towards total development of children. He was democratic in his approach. Being from the field of guidance, unlike the previous Principal, he believed in self-discipline, working leadership and instead of lop-sided academic studies he laid stress on multi-dimensional development of children. As he started functioning in the school, taking everybody together, his vibrant and beaming personality motivated and enthused staff and students alike. It was a treat to find the same teachers rejuvenated into action driven by the Principal's call for collective thinking and excellence in performance. Frequent meetings at all levels, academic innovations and discussions and participatory approach helped to developed mutual trust and regard between the teachers and the Principal. He structured a pro forma to collect biodata of each teacher along with information about each person's interest in identified activities with which they would like to be associated. Based on the responses to the schedule, an annual plan of activities was developed at the beginning of the session followed by month wise and week wise calendar for the year.

While under the new leadership, academic studies went on with same vigour, significant changes were brought about in the school curriculum. The school was again affiliated to the Central Board of Secondary Education, New Delhi.

- A teacher's diary was introduced. It was to be submitted every Monday, indicating teaching plans for the whole week. The Principal used to check each one of them personally.
- The school was divided into six Houses, each under the charge of a House master and a House captain. Regular House meetings were held and activities, competitions and field trips were organised.
- Science, social science and commerce clubs were formed. These clubs were mainly academic in nature. Club meetings were regularly held wherein members planned and organised various co-curricular activities.
- Participation of the school in science fairs, debates, intra- and inter-school competitions became a regular feature. The school started participating in state and national science airs and earned distinctions. Even the science teacher earned laurels for the school at National Science Fair.
- The morning prayer was remodelled to include:
    - o All religious prayers on Fridays;
    - o Dress, cleanliness and hygiene checks every day
    - o Prayers both in English and Hindi;

  - o Motivational talks and talks on moral themes every day by Principal and teachers
  - o Reading news by students in both Hindi and English
  - o Mass PT and yoga once in a week.
- A zero period was carved out in the school time table for conducting a variety of literary and cultural activities
- A comprehensive Work Experience Programme was chalked out and implemented meticulously in wood work, metal work, electronics, commerce, home science and agriculture.
- Students' book store, students' bank, school kitchen garden, aquarium and provision of freshly prepared food items during lunch hours are only a few innovative work experience projects managed and run by students.
- Further, an 'earn while you learn' scheme was developed in wood work. Under this scheme, many utility items were manufactured and sold. Also, dual desks and benches were prepared for the entire school. Even some class IV employees along with needy students of the school, volunteered after school hours.
- A scheme of continuous and comprehensive evaluation was put into practice. An annual plan of activity was followed meticulously, wherein every child and teacher participated in one activity or the other. Rating scales were used to grade the children on their performance.

Apart from the above following innovative ideas were successfully practised in the school:

Spontaneous Value Inculcation through School Diary

A very novel method of inculcating values in students was introduced by the Principal. For this innovative practice, each child was provided with a specially designed school diary at the beginning of the session. Each diary contained few pages especially meant for making anecdotal notes by teachers. Students were informed that every child enrolled in the school had been initially awarded 100 marks to their credit. Based on the nature of their conduct demonstrated at various points of time during the year, they could either improve the score by showing exemplary behaviour or let it go down the scale by indulging in unsocial activities. In the said pages of the diary, there were columns where any teacher could record +5, +10, +15 or any positive numeral in consonance with the intensity and nature of the good conduct demonstrated by the child within or outside the school. Similarly, negative marks were recorded for any bad or unacceptable conduct.

At the end of the academic session, all diaries were collected and the final score for each child was calculated by adding or subtracting the marks obtained, similar to the calculations done in a savings bank account passbook. Based on the final balance, students were awarded one, two or three stars at the annual function of the school. The norms for these awards were worked out collectively viz., a child raising their marks to 150 and above but less than 200 got one star; a child with 200 and above but less than 250 got two stars, And a child raising their balance to 250 but less than 300 got three stars. This mode of recognition and adding or subtracting of marks brought a perceptible change in the social and personal behaviour of the children. They became highly motivated to demonstrate socially acceptable and commendable behaviour in their day-to-day interactions with elders, peers and the needy.

As a result of this innovation, disciplined and civilised behaviour permeated the whole school environment. The children not only became extremely cautious about their behaviour but also, a few children were found bitterly weeping even if 1 (one) negative mark was recorded by the teacher.

Cleanliness and Beautification

Another innovative experience was related to the cleanliness and beautification of the campus and its surroundings with active participation of students and teachers. The objective of this innovative project was to encourage children to take the initiative, share responsibility collectively and develop aesthetic appreciation among students. The implementation of the project ultimately led to healthy competition and, at the same time, helped in improving the cleanliness and beautification of the school premises, including classrooms, corridors, entrances, parks, playgrounds and prayer grounds. The process was like this:

The whole school premise was divided among the Houses, such that each House received equal share of the said space. Cleanliness and beautification of each identified portion was the responsibility of the identified House. Each portion was provided with big-size display boards, flannel boards and big photographs in addition to building spaces, parks or gardens. Each House every week used to put up informative features on contemporary topics, displayed their own creations and collections and used their ingenuity to keep clean and beautify their allotted areas.

On every Saturday, a jury consisting of the coordinator, a senior PGT and the Principal used to go round and assess the performance of each House on a predetermined criterion. On following Monday, the rankings were announced in the prayer assembly amidst clapping from students. The House captain of the House getting the highest rank, was then invited by the Principal to hoist the flag of his own House in the forefront of the prayer ground. The flag of the House continued to remain hoisted for the complete week. Prayer assembly under the flag of the highest ranking House signified the recognition by the school community of its best performance.

It was quite interesting to note that this symbolic recognition became so prestigious among the Houses that each one began using newer approaches to improve its performance, resulting in clean and beautiful surroundings week after week. The matter did not end here. In fact, marks obtained by each House got added by the year's end and were used to select the 'Best House' for awarding the winning shield.

Games for All

Another innovative activity named 'games for all' was tried out. The school, being a day school was almost entirely dependent on buses to fetch and drop back children, it was not feasible to organise games in the evening. So it was thought to have a block period every week devoted to games for all. During this long period, it was compulsory for every child and teacher to be in the open and participate in one or the other outdoor game.

School Experiment Brings Amazing Social Change

At a time when the city did not even have a single poultry unit or the egg eating habit among its population, the school started a small demonstration poultry farm. Agriculture teachers, under the direction of American consultants, motivated students opting for agriculture as a stream, to start small home projects in poultry on their respective rooftops. This small beginning by the school in early sixties was picked up initially by a local doctor. His entrepreneurial venture in the vicinity of the school gave rise to a chain reaction of investment in poultry industry by insiders as well as outsiders. Today the city boasts of investment to the tune of crores of rupees. So much so, that the city today has achieved the distinction of being one of the largest suppliers of eggs in the whole region.

Professional Development of Teachers

In these days of rising aspirations, professional development of teachers has gained utmost importance. Apart from individual efforts, the school too has a responsibility to positively contribute in this direction. Any initiative by the school to orient, refresh, motivate or provide opportunities for unfolding of inherent talents not only helps in the professional growth of the teacher but also leads to a general improvement of the academic atmosphere of the school and, consequently, the teaching performance.

The Principal, in this case, motivated teachers to take up action research projects. On his suggestion, a forum named Educational Research Associates (ERA) was formed. Its doors were open for any teacher who wanted to join on a voluntary basis. Initially, only five out of about forty-eight teachers came forward. They held regular meetings in which research papers were presented, new projects were planned, presented and discussed, research-based interventions were thought of and implemented. The success of ERA can be judged from the fact that four of the five teachers won National Awards under the Seminar Readings Programme of the NCERT. One of them rose to the post of Professor and Principal, while one became Reader and two, Lecturers at the college level. Yet another teacher from that group later received National Award for Best Teacher.

Interestingly, it was surprising to find that these innovative projects and activities had no adverse effect on the annual results of the school. On the contrary Board's certificates of merit were still won. Also, the school achieved distinction in co-curricular activities at the state and national levels. Each student of the school became a moving ambassador through his multi–dimensional traits, conduct and achievements. This was reflected in the following year's enrolment, which once again picked up. To everyone's surprise, enrolment again crossed the 1000 mark within a span of three years. Ultimately the Principal had to face strong pressure from higher authorities/MLAs for giving admission to children as recommended by them.

The success story of this school hopefully will motivate many educators to innovate new projects, new ways of teaching, better ways of enforcing discipline, ensuring vertical mobility of teachers and enhancing the possibility of multi-dimensional growth and development of learners. In this age of digital technology, online courses, video conferencing, use of social media and internet, there is ample scope for worthwhile innovations. The need is only to have a right attitude, using imagination and bringing newer ideas into practice.

Reference

NCERT (1966) Report of the National Commission on Education (1964-66) New Delhi, Govt. of India.

GOI,MHRD. National Education Policy, 2020, 5.23,page 22, New Delhi.

9
An Experiment in Peer Evaluation

Genesis of the Project

Evaluation is an integral component of any curriculum. Every teacher evaluates students to judge the extent of learning outcomes achieved by them. As a matter of fact, everyone in this world, at some point of time or the other evaluates himself. Similarly, people often judge those with whom they meet or interact in day-to-day life. Statements like *How do I look like? What do others think about me? He is making a fool of himself. 'He should behave in a more responsible manner'* are very common. Apparently, these may look like isolated comments, but in fact, systematic observation and judgment are at the base of each such statement. It is through such evaluations/ peer judgments that we often ask ourselves, *How can I perform better*? and thereby, we tend to modify ourselves.

Everyone has a basic urge to receive recognition from others. We often seek others' comments on the task performed or to be performed. In this age of social media, people post on WhatsApp, Facebook, Instagram and Twitter to get likes and comments. They share their joy of success or even sorrow, as it is a human tendency to get elated on being noticed by others, on receiving praise or positive comments.

In our scriptures, much has been said about the effect of *Sangati* or impact of peer group. Good and enlightened *sangati*/ peer group often changes lives for better. Conversely, bad *sangati* / peer group is capable of ruining the lives of promising young persons. It is on this premise that Ability Sections have been organised in institutions. Students with enriched interactions with peers not only excel in studies but also decide their future course of action, namely their entry into higher or professional education and, subsequently, their future career based on their interactions with more knowledgeable peers. The concept of cooperative learning is also based on the fact that students learn faster and better when their peers assist them in studies. Monitorial systems, focus group discussions, interactive learning and the like are some variations in this context. As a matter of fact, faculty seminars, peer evaluation, faculty confluence and special enrichment sessions are promoted and regularly organised on the basic premise that we learn by mutual interaction and shared experiences in a social context.

Taking a cue from these experiences and for utilising opportunities to learn from each other as well as to bring about improvements in teaching based on peer observations, suggestions and mutual interactions, an innovative project was planned and implemented in collaboration with the faculty members in a College of Education in Gurugram under the directions of the author. The objectives of the project were as follows:

- To create an inner urge among faculty members to improve
- To develop trust and an innovative mindset among the faculty members
- To develop objective observation skills for identifying the strengths and weaknesses of a transacted lesson
- To judge the extent and quality of learner participation, teacher–pupil interaction, appropriateness of the teaching methodology and the overall classroom climate
- To suggest alternative strategies and steps for further improvement.

Before Implementation

Introducing peer evaluation was easy to conceive but difficult to deliver. It was, in fact, a challenge since it involved judging the effectiveness of the lesson delivered by a peer by observing the lesson, followed by writing candid remarks on the given pro forma. Since it was reciprocal, the chances of bias creeping in were real. A number of faculty meetings were held to thrash out all conflicting viewpoints. After much persuasion, the faculty members got convinced that the project was an academic exercise with the positive intention of introducing improvement in their teaching. They were assured that peer inputs will be openly discussed, resulting in suitable modifications in the planning and presentation of the lesson. The project was initiated only after it was accepted by everyone wholeheartedly.

College Level Implementation

The innovative project of peer evaluation/observation among faculty members in the said College of Education was introduced in the year 2009. The project successfully continued till 2012 (four years). Every day during this period, faculty members in groups of two were assigned mutual classes for observation and submission of their objective and subjective responses to the Director (Author). This continued for all the four academic sessions.

Feedback

The feedback thus obtained was compiled after due scrutiny and discussion. The experiment worked quite well when implemented after due preparation. In fact, it proved to be a blessing in disguise since faculty members reported that they have thereafter become more conscious about the instructional objectives, classroom climate, interaction pattern and the question-answer technique used, thus improving the effectiveness of their teaching in the process. Views of the faculty were systematically obtained, which are summarised as follows:

- The experiment developed amongst us an interest for doing something innovative in teaching methodology
- Reflections of our ideas, most of the time were seen executed in the subsequent peer presentations
- We got familiarised with the diversified approaches of teaching
- The direct effect of the methodology used can be seen on students and their achievement
- 'How to make lessons interactive with effective classroom management?' was understood

- We got acquainted with effective use of different aids in teaching–learning process
- While observing peer-teaching, student's behaviour was observed that provided an impetus to make lesson effective
- Feedback received was helpful in improving the shortcomings

Collection of Data

In order to collect data, an Observation Schedule was finalised after due discussion. However, after the first trial, it was felt that the objectives of the innovation would be better achieved if some subjective/qualitative inputs were also received along with objective remarks. With this in view, Part A of the Observation Schedule was supplemented by Part B and added to the schedule. The schedule, therefore, now consisted of, in addition to closed observation items, some open-ended questions like 'If you were to teach the same lesson over again, how would you introduce the lesson? Which additional teaching aids would you use? Which examples or illustrations are likely to make the lesson more effective? What was the overall reaction of the students to the lesson? Give your critical assessment of the lesson/the peer you observed.

This was done to obtain a critical feedback in a subjective manner. The faculty also graded each lesson observed on a five-point scale, viz: A – Excellent; B – Very good; C – Good; D – Fair; E – Needs improvement. Each faculty was also asked to suggest alternative strategy/strategies to transact the lesson to make it more effective. Finally, the given format emerged for peer evaluation/observation and was used for collecting the required data.

Peer Observation Pro Forma

Part A

i. General Particulars

Name of the faculty:

Class :	Section :	Period :	Time :
Subject :	Topic :	Date :	

No. of students :

Part A
ii. Specific Observations

Dimension	Category	Sub-Category	Observation
Classroom transaction	Entering the class	With greeting/smiling/grave/serious/pleasant mood/irritating mood	
	Beginning the lesson	Introducing the lesson, indirect/ direct approach	
	Methodology used	Asking questions, showing charts, cards, writing on blackboard, one child or teacher does and others repeat, reading, explaining, correcting, demonstration, use of ICT–PPT, video, graphics	
	Teaching-learning material	Teacher made/student made, TLM Used	
	Reinforcement	Positive/negative	
	Kind of activity teachers expect from the children in the class	Listen to the teacher attentively, answer questions posed by the teacher, copy from book, copy from blackboard, participate in discussion	
	Homework/ assignment	Writing, learning, problem-solving	
	Ending the lesson	Recapitulation, activity-based, abrupt writing work	
Classroom climate	Organisation and management	Good (organised, warm/friendly, supportive, pleasant, accepting, encouraging, helpful), bad (chaotic, disorganised, cold, unfriendly, threatening, rigidly controlled)	
	About the lesson	Most significant and important part, relevance to life, accuracy, interesting examples given	
	Teacher's movement in the classroom	Amount of time spent in one section of the room, amount of time spent in one place, amount of time utilised in going around the class	
	Discipline	Rigid, lassies-faire, liberal	
Teacher–pupil interaction	Style of addressing children	Individually, by name, as a whole (group), pointing finger at the child, using derogatory words (Hey, *Suno*)	

Dimension	Category	Sub-Category	Observation
	Questions asked by the teacher	Subject-related questions, experience-related questions, questions asking to write, read and draw, asking children for their participation, asking children to repeat and clarify doubts, teacher asking general questions, asking students about their life outside school.	
	Answers of children	All together in chorus, correct answer, wrong answer, teacher helps them in answering/ correcting could not answer, passive listener, teaches and gives no chance to answer	
	Instruction given by the teacher	Subject-related, discipline-related, clues given by the teacher: verbal, non-verbal (physical)	
Participation	Seeking children's attention and involvement in the classroom	Rapport building, voice modulation, resourcefulness, reinforcement	
	Types of vocal expressions of the students	Asking something, shouting/weeping, complaining, talking, explaining, making noise, whispering	
	Participation of the students	Students answer, answer in chorus, not paying attention and doing something else, students respond positively to the teacher's instructions, students don't answer	
Building emotional climate	Developing student's self-confidence	Helps students feel capable, minimises the effect of making mistakes, builds confidence, focuses on improvement, shows faith in students, acknowledges the difficulty of tasks, focuses on past success, recognises achievement, applauses, acknowledges successful experiences	
	Helping students to interact and become involved with others	Acceptance (accepts sincerely and unconditionally, accepts student's personal style), attention (greets/listens to students, spends time chatting, involvement in the project with students), appreciation, affirmation (acknowledges the positive traits verbally or in writing), affection (showing affection while things go bad), showing kindness	
	Help students contribute	Encourages students, invites students' help with daily tasks, encourages students to help other students, promotes group activity	
Evaluation	Exercise/assignment	Given question, assignment, task or project: individual or group	

Part B

1. Please grade the lesson delivered on a five-point scale: A, B, C, D or E (A – Excellent; B – Very good; C – Good; D – Fair; E – Needs improvement)
2. Suggest alternative strategy/strategies to transact the lesson to make it more effective.

   ____

   ____

   ____

3. If you were to teach the same lesson over again:
   - How will you introduce the lesson?
   - Which alternative teaching aids would you prefer?
   - Which additional examples or illustrations are likely to make the lesson more comprehensible?

   ____

   ____

   ____

4. How was the overall reaction of the students to the lesson?

   ____

   ____

   ____

5. Give your critical assessment of the lesson/ the peer you observed.

   ____

   ____

   ____

It may be seen that in addition to closed observations, some open-ended questions were added. This was done to obtain a critical feedback in a subjective manner.

As regards resources, the author provided a set of schedules/ pro forma as shown earlier to each faculty. A time schedule indicating names of concerned faculty members was made available every day. The innovative practice was disseminated through college souvenir for wider information. Visitors from other institutions visiting the College of Education were apprised of the practice. It has been highly appreciated by them.

The exercise is just an example to show that a teacher educator can devise simple experiments to motivate, improve and give new experiences to student–teachers. Such experiments not only bring freshness but also go a long way in creating a culture of research and innovation in the institution.

10
Experimentation in Teacher Education in India

In India, *acharya, guru or teacher* is given more importance than even God because it is the guru who can show us the way to realise God. (*Guru Govind Dono Khare Kaake Laagoon Pai, Balihari Guru Aapno Jin Govind Dio Bataya).* This *guru–shishya parampara*, continued in India for thousands of years. It continued during Moghul Empire as *ustad–shaagird* tradition. But it was in the British period that the present-day version of teacher–students–classroom model took the stage and the spread of education further widened. After political independence, the process of democratising education began with greater earnest. Historically speaking, in post-independent India, we come across wide-ranging recommendations of a number of commissions and committees on education. These *inter alia* made specific recommendations for transforming the teacher education programme in the country to make it professional, flexible, digital and oriented to the contemporary needs. Education Commission (1964-66) maintained that "the essence of a programme of teacher education is 'quality' and in its absence, teacher education becomes not only a financial waste but source of the overall deterioration in educational standards" NCERT (1966). With the establishment of the National Council for Teacher Education (NCTE) as a statutory body for regulating and enhancing the quality of teacher education in the country, fresh thinking started on the subject. The NCTE documents and stipulations have generated much debate and discussion regarding the efficacy and effectiveness of existing teacher education programmes, including their quality and adequacy for professional preparation. All stakeholders today are keeping a close watch on the developments aimed at consolidating the gains and discouraging the commercialisation of teacher education.

Some Important Experiments

After independence, based on the recommendations of education commissions and committees, the country witnessed many well-meaning experiments and innovations in teacher education. These were aimed at producing competent and committed teachers who could help shape the destiny of the free democratic country. The country considered education as the most potent instrument of change. It realised that the pace of developing an egalitarian society based on non-discrimination, social justice, equity and equality can be accelerated only by providing the right type of education. Some experiments like the four-year teacher education programme continues even today in some universities. Recently, the National Education Policy 2020 stated that "All stand-alone TEIs will be required to convert to multidisciplinary institutions by 2025 and offer the 4-year integrated teacher preparation programme. All large multidisciplinary universities—including all public universities as well as all Model Multidisciplinary Colleges shall establish, develop and house outstanding education departments which, aside from carrying out cutting-edge research in various aspects of education, will also run B.Ed. programmes to educate future teachers. The 4-year integrated B.Ed. offered by such multidisciplinary HEIs will, by 2030, become the minimal degree qualification for school teachers. The 4-year integrated B.Ed. will be a dual-major holistic Bachelor's degree in Education as well as a specialised subject (such as a language, history, music, mathematics, computer science, chemistry, economics, etc.)".

Besides the four-year programmes, experiments were carried out with teacher education programmes of different durations and by offering different specialisations, but many of these have been forgotten. Further, no systematic evaluations have been undertaken to identify their strengths and weaknesses.

Consequently, these experiments got phased out without drawing worthwhile lessons from them for the future. An effort, therefore, is being made in this book to document these experiments made at the national level with a view to generate a long-term and informed viewpoint to professionalise and diversify the teacher education programme in the years to come.

Establishment of Regional Colleges

In pursuance of the recommendations of the Secondary Education Commission (1952–53), the then Ministry of Education, Government of India, in collaboration with the Ohio State University, USA, established four Regional Colleges of Education in four regions of the country. The catchment area for each college was delimited to a specific region of the country, for example, Regional College at Ajmer for the northern region, Bhopal for the western region, Mysore for the southern region and Bhubaneswar for the eastern region. These colleges continue even today as regional institutes with a much wider academic scope and revamped curricula. Incidentally, a new regional institute has been added in Shillong, subsequently catering to the northeastern region of the country.

Initially, the faculty members in the four regional colleges were oriented in the Ohio State University and consultants from the university assisted the college in implementing the 'plan and programme' produced specifically for the purpose. These colleges were envisaged as the pace-setting teacher education institutions for the country. Each college had a 'demonstration school' attached to it within the campus. These colleges, in the beginning, were mandated to prepare teachers for the Multipurpose Scheme recommended by the Mudaliar Commission. Each college was affiliated to the respective state university for the award of degree with the understanding that the colleges would be autonomous as regards their curriculum and could terminate or start new courses as per the needs of the region. All innovations were to be tried out in the attached demonstration schools before canvassing these in the region. Both the college and school in each region experimented with many novel ideas and are doing so even today.

Four-Year Integrated Courses

The regional colleges started with a four-year integrated course leading to the degree of Bachelor of Technical Education (BTechEd) in the early sixties. This course initially proposed as BSc (Tech) BEd was aimed at preparing technical teachers for multipurpose schools. The course in its final form offered two specialisations, namely in Engineering Science and Engineering Trade. The syllabus for each of the four years was meticulously planned. It included languages, general studies and social sciences integrated aptly along with science and technology. Content and pedagogy were meshed in appropriate proportions in the four-year curriculum. Compulsory games and sports, fully residential complex for both students and faculty, state of the art library with open access system, compulsory educational tour for students in the final year to other regions of the country, provision of nationally selected best faculty and fully equipped laboratories and workshops and stipend to students ultimately evolved into a rigorously implemented comprehensive curriculum. It was a balanced mix of scholastic and co-scholastic activities, games and sports, internship in teaching, cultural and recreational activities.

Since the scheme of multipurpose schools was shelved by the time the first batch of BTechEd students were thrown into the job market, most of the pass outs were left to fend for themselves. Surprisingly, the first and second-batch students who pursued this integrated curriculum proved to be most successful in their lives. The alumni made a mark of their own wherever they got placed. Their placement list is quite diverse and long. Those who entered a school or college as a teacher, demonstrators or junior lecturers excelled in their positions and simultaneously improved their qualifications to become professors and principals. Some of them even reached the top positions in the hierarchy. Some got placements in polytechnics and engineering colleges, others chose to work in industries industry and retired as managers or inspectors, and still, others worked in banks and public sector undertakings like railways, telecommunications and research organisations. Unfortunately, only two batches graduated with the original curriculum. With the third batch, the syllabus was revamped and enriched mainly to provide mobility with AMIE. Consequently, the engineering content was un-proportionately enhanced to give a clear engineering bias to the curriculum, thereby substantially eliminating humanities and science components. This was deliberately done so that students could get placements in polytechnics and engineering colleges and move on after undergoing AMIE. The strategy adopted was basically to make up for the absence of multipurpose schools. This change, however, was neither welcomed by the students who could hardly cope with the content nor by the engineering colleges. The latter did not accept the students for their teaching positions for reasons best known to them. As a result, a versatile teacher education programme died its tragic death but not before it gave many lessons to the posterity.

We have two more examples of four-year teacher education programmes in this context. One is again from regional institutes of education, i.e., B.A., B.Ed.—a four-year integrated course to prepare social science and humanities teachers. This course also has been highly acclaimed in the field, which is obvious from the fact that it had to be restarted after it was closed down following the recommendations of expert committee. The second four-year programme comes from one of the progressive universities, namely Delhi University, which has floated the B.EI.Ed. Programme—a four-year integrated course to prepare elementary teachers for the system. Maharshi Dayanand University, Rohtak, also experimented with the programme in KIIT College of Education, Gurugram, under the direction and supervision of the Author. It was, however, short-lived in Haryana, where two-year D.Ed. programme received preference from the students. Yet another course that was started in the sixties but continues even today with many modifications is the four-year integrated course in science education, namely BSc BEd It is going on in all the regional colleges, now known as Regional Institutes of Education under the overall administration of NCERT.

Although four-year teacher education programmes have remained a significant model for preparing teachers in the US, these have not yet caught the imagination of education management in India. The success achieved by the products of the four-year courses of B.Sc., B.Ed., B.A., B.Ed. and also the versatility of the earlier four-year course of B.Tech.Ed. have amply proved that teacher preparation requires longer time, enriched curriculum, suitable environment, up to date human and material resources along with a farsighted management. Teaching requires individuals who take teaching as a mission of their lives right from the beginning. This is possible when they are caught young and have prolonged interaction, enriched exposure and an imaginatively developed dynamic curriculum. The latter should provide sustained theoretical and practical work, a value-based environment and intensive periods of internship in the schools.

Incidentally, I happen to be the product of the first batch of the four-year course of B.Tech.Ed. My experience of over 50 years in NCERT and KIIT, Gurugram today tells me that young students who enter the teacher education course just after their higher secondary or intermediate and gradually imbibe the qualities and characteristics of a teacher through content cum pedagogy training, definitely shape into committed, competent and conscientious teachers.

Specialised BEd Programmes

The regional institutes also earlier experimented with three-year teacher education programmes leading to Diploma in Industrial Arts and Crafts and two-year M.Sc.Ed. courses in physical and biological sciences for producing teachers for the higher secondary classes. Other experiments in innovative teacher education programmes included one year specialised B.Ed. programmes, namely B.Ed. (agriculture), B.Ed. (home science), B.Ed. (languages), B.Ed. (science), B.Ed. (vocational), etc. The products of these courses have been well received by the mainstream education system. Over the years, many more experiments have been launched. For instance, there is a pre-service teacher education programme of two years going on in DIETs for preparing elementary teachers. The training programmes of BTC and D.Ed., D.EC.Ed., D.EI.Ed., D.P.Ed., B.P.Ed., M.P.Ed. and teacher education through ODL are other variations in this context. In other words, teacher education programmes experimented upon till date have varied durations ranging from one to four years.

Correspondence Courses

Many universities in the late seventies started correspondence courses on teacher education for working teachers. But these were shabbily planned and very loosely implemented in terms of course work, continuous monitoring and evaluation. These resulted in degeneration of correspondence courses into money-making propositions. Understandably, as soon as the NCTE became a statutory body, the initial euphoria led to the closure of all correspondence courses without even systematically assessing their need and lacunae in planning or implementation. Absence of any viable alternative to correspondence courses led to the recent unfortunate phenomenon of 'non-attending' students. A probe into the reasons for being 'non-attending' led to the following facts in one such state:

- Boys and girls working in private schools but desirous of getting a B.Ed. degree do not have any provision for study leave, paid or unpaid
- Newly married women at the reproductive age and lactating mothers aspiring to become a teacher are not in a position to leave home for long durations. Also, they cannot commute long distances due to poor transport facilities, especially in rural and semi-urban areas
- Girls are keen to study, but are not allowed to attend classes by the family for obvious reasons
- Working boys and girls in other professions desirous to enter the teaching profession.

One can recollect the correspondence courses run by the regional colleges of education under NCERT during the sixties and seventies. In these summer courses, correspondence and contact modes were judiciously mixed and the correspondence course material was meticulously prepared, mailed, monitored and evaluated. These courses are remembered even today as the ones that helped the working teachers in transforming themselves into effective teachers for the system.

The need, in fact, was to reform the correspondence courses by revamping those using rigorous checks and balances instead of their instant closure.

Two-year-BEd Programme—Need for Fresh Thinking

A significant innovation in teacher education was suggested by the NCTE (1998) in its Teacher Education Framework. This was related to enhancing the duration of B.Ed. course to two years from the prevailing one year duration and simultaneously enriching its content and process. I had the opportunity to initiate the two-year B.Ed. programme in the Regional Institute of Education, Bhopal, first as its Dean and continued later as its Principal. A research paper of mine published in 'University News' (Sen Gupta, et. al, 2002) clearly indicated the difference the two-year programme had made in the attitude and behaviour of students due to intensive training and extensive school exposure. A significant finding of the study stated that "An overwhelming majority (92%) were confident that they would gain proficiency in content and methodology after completing the two-year curriculum". But unfortunately, except NCERT's regional institutes, no other institution or university in the country replicated the well-thought-out reform till NCTE, using legal provisions, extended the duration for B.Ed. course in general from one to two years with revamped curriculum.

Subsequently, the National Education Policy 2020 further extended the duration to four years with enriched curriculum for professional preparation of teachers. As and when the policy is implemented, four-year teacher education courses will become the norm. However, the policy also talks of retaining 2-year course for specialised training. "The 2-year B.Ed. programmes will also be offered by the same multidisciplinary institutions offering the 4-year integrated B.Ed., and will be intended only for those who have already obtained Bachelor's Degrees in other specialised subjects. These B.Ed. programmes may also be replaced by suitably adapted 1-year B.Ed. programmes, and will be offered only to those who have completed the equivalent of 4-year multidisciplinary Bachelor's Degrees or who have obtained a Master's degree in a speciality and wish to become a subject teacher in that speciality." (NEP, 2020)

Keeping in view the ground realities wherein two-year B.Ed. programme definitely gave better results than B.Ed. one year the suggestion is that let it transform itself into specialised B.Ed. programmes for preparing teachers for higher secondary subjects like computer science, physics, chemistry, economics and the like through content cum pedagogy curriculum. Specialised programmes can also be formulated for engineering, management or home science and other such specialised subjects. Obviously, in such courses content of the subject will be specially transacted through specific discipline-based pedagogy. The degree awarded at the completion of this specialised course can be B. Ed. (Hons) in a given specialisation. Till date, there are no tailor-made teacher education courses catering to different subjects at the higher secondary stage and post-higher secondary stages. These programmes, if properly implemented, will not only raise the performance level of students but will also become a game changer for bringing in quality into higher education.

Conclusion

The account given in this chapter shows that although the response to any change is very slow in our system, and hence sometimes termed as anti-change and rigid, there have been positive overtures from the schools towards worthwhile experiments and innovations in the past. The system, however, lacks a research mindset. Many futuristic decisions are taken without systematically assessing the existing schemes with a view to introduce correctives for plugging the loopholes. Many beneficial programmes in the past have come and gone for reasons other than the potential and need of the programme. It is easy to abandon a programme, but it is difficult to redesign it taking lessons from the past.

As indicated earlier, a need is now being felt for specialised teacher education programmes at the post-secondary stage for diversified and skill based vocational courses in computer, engineering education, science education, language education, humanities, home science and management education. Therefore, a comprehensive policy of teacher education is urgently required in the country. The university system should come forward with new models of teacher education to meet the newer avenues being generated by the knowledge society of tomorrow. Let us face the questions: 'Are we preparing students for coping with the newer opportunities in the developing economy? Are we utilising the new digital technology for organising SMART classes and creating curious minds and developing creative democratic citizens of tomorrow? In fact, the preparation of a professional teacher for multi-specialisation, is a long-drawn process particularly when it means transforming their attitude, mental outlook and work culture along with mastery of the subject matter. The scope of teacher education needs to be expanded by bringing in more and more specialisations while retaining the human aspects that a living teacher brings to the classroom.

References

NCTE (1998) Policy Perspectives in Teacher Education, National Council for Teacher Education, New Delhi.

Government of India, Ministry of Education (1952-53) Report of the Secondary Education Commission, New Delhi.

NCERT (1966) Report of the National Commission on Education (1964-66). New Delhi: Govt. of India.

Sen Gupta, M., Kakariya, V.K. & Chugtai, I. B. (2002) Two-Year B. Ed. Programme: An Experiment in Quality Teacher Education. *University News*, 40 (45) 11–17, New Delhi.

11

Teacher–Student Relationship at Tertiary Stage

Teacher–student relationship attains special significance, especially at the post-secondary stage. It is the time when students come out of the protected environment of a school and, for the first time, start enjoying the open atmosphere of a college or university. Also, boys and girls at the age of 17 or 18 pass through a transition period when they move from leisure-faire adolescence to responsible adulthood. At this late adolescent period, children swing in a dream world. They have high aspirations, which at times may even be unrealistic. Play of emotions is in abundance in their lives. They display carefree attitude in the face of most difficult problems. During this volatile period, they occasionally experience a strong desire to accomplish something great, achieve targets that look impossible and often intend to attain immediate visibility. Simultaneously, they also experience a force of drag in whatever they do due to a feeling of uncertainty of future combined with parental pressure to achieve more. Of course, financial constraints too add to the problems. However, physical limitations and accompanying drag or negative factors need not always be frustrating. These, at times, work as motivating factors. However, it depends on the personality make-up of a person, his attitude towards life and also the type and nature of advice received from friends and elders.

As said earlier, during school days, children remain under constant surveillance and guidance. But as the child enters the portals of a college they experience a totally different kind of atmosphere. This atmosphere is comparatively free and permissive. There are very few restrictions. Students, by and large, have to take their own decisions. Although there will be too many friends but their reliability always poses a question mark when it comes to depending on them for taking day-to-day decisions. The new entrants face temptations that are too alluring or difficult to resist. In such a situation, they are found roaming in a rudderless boat, but they hardly feel a desire to come out of this whirlpool. These young adolescents need proper direction and emotional support from a trustworthy friend or a compassionate guide. Here comes the need and importance of a mature and experienced teacher to fill the void. The personality of this teacher has to be fully composed, more of a fatherly figure on whom students can depend and confide.

In our colleges and universities, professors have an image of being sophisticated, research minded and most of the time involved in academic pursuits. Students, particularly the new ones, find the teachers to be confined to themselves. They prefer to maintain a safe distance from students. On being approached, many a time, teachers comment, 'you are no longer a child'.

At this crucial juncture, these new entrants require patronage and support. In free and democratic environs, amidst the fear of getting ragged by the seniors, college teachers should not persist with this snobbish mentality. They must reach out to these young students, converse with them as friends and make every effort to create a healthy relationships especially for those who are new to this kind of free and permissive atmosphere.

The basic conditions for maintaining a healthy relationship between two persons may be summed up as follows:

- having equal status;
- have same or similar goals to achieve
- working in same organisation
- Sharing the same language, customs or traditions.

Therefore, when it is a question of cultivating a healthy relationship between the teacher and the student, obviously, the teacher has to reach out to the student and take the initiative to develop confidence in him. They have to find ways and means to instill in students a sense of security. Students have to be helped to develop confidence and commitment towards better adjustment. There are many ways to do so. For example, teachers and students together may organise get-togethers, celebrate common functions, organise welcome parties, induction programme, literary and cultural programmes, and exchange of ideas and display of talents. In this task of rapport-building to create a feel of homeliness amongst new entrants, teacher counsellors, house masters, HODs, hostel wardens, proctorial/ disciplinary board members and staff advisors can play a crucial role by facilitating wider participation in such friendly events by offering opportunities for interactions amongst seniors and new entrants thereby developing mutual relationships. However, it would be essential to keep a keen eye to prevent any untoward incident or going to extremes.

Right from day one every faculty member should converse freely with as many students as possible. In other words, channels of communication should remain open with both old and new students. This would help in taking preventive measures and also guiding them to more constructive pursuits. Right from the beginning of the session, students should be engaged in activities which will acclimatise them with the new set-up. These may be in the form of feature or documentary film shows, exposure to the English language through film shows, videos or audio programmes, expert presentations on career opportunities, talent search and a well-planned induction programme. The induction programme for newcomers may focus on–institutional philosophy—its vision and mission, learning environment, university/college academic traditions, achievements, requirements of discipline, attendance, faculty and its expectations and exemplary stories of alumni.

It is advisable to involve students, through different committees, in drafting activities, and drawing out a calendar of activities—literary, cultural, games, sports, gymnastics, yoga and so on. Relationship with students needs to be carefully cultivated and nurtured within the faculty and amongst different faculties. While relationship between teacher and student will be characterised by warmth and closeness, at the same time, utmost care has to be taken to maintain a safe distance to keep the awe alive. However, students should feel free to share their personal problems with the teacher. But they must always have a subtle feeling of fear of authority, which is essential to curb indiscipline. In other words, a teacher should become a counsellor, guide and friend to the students.

It is the duty of the teacher to moderate in students the quality of their aspirations and raise them from mere egoistic state to the state of consciousness. The teacher, through his supportive behaviour, presents before the students a living example of inner integrity, character and mastery of knowledge. The conscientious teacher always feels concern for the safety, security and welfare of his students. Such a teacher never shows arrogance or a sense of superiority. On the contrary, they let students practise self-control, be independent in their thinking and enable them to share responsibilities.

In this context, relevant questions to ponder are:

- Why do students indulge in ragging?
- What do they gain by doing so?
- Whether this distortion in behaviour is because of any deficiency in their way of rearing at home?
- Has it something to do with the education received at school?
- Does education breed hatred and violence and not human values and social qualities?
- How far are social stratification and politico-social factors responsible for inhuman behaviour?
- How to transform their thinking process?
- Why do they indulge in violence in the name of ragging?

Reasons may vary from situation to situation. Disappearance of the joint family system and emergence of nuclear families may be an important reason leading to selfishness and aggressiveness in children. Devoid of opportunities at home, they lack in displaying the feelings of sharing and caring. Cutthroat competition all around for achieving superiority gives a push to hatred and violence. Violence highlighted in print and non-print media further adds fuel to the fire. However, it is the teaching community that should research in a particular context and find answers to the above-stated questions, so that they can take remedial measures for doing away with any kind of violence or mental torture to new entrants.

12
Towards Humanistic Teacher Education

Teacher educators often fail to appreciate that a programme of teacher education does not simply relate to content and its pedagogy. In the ultimate analysis, it is the process of preparing a human being to become a sensitive person, a good citizen, an efficient facilitator having vital personal qualities of empathy, understanding and respect for human dignity. This is possible only when due focus is given upon the development of the persona of the teacher. In other words, it would require primary attention towards the development of right feelings, attitudes, opinions and beliefs of the teacher during the formative phase of the teacher education programme. In a similar vein, National Education Policy (NEP) 2020 has articulated that "Teacher education is truly vital in creating a team of school teachers that will shape the next generation. Teacher preparation is an activity that requires multidisciplinary perspectives and knowledge, the formation of dispositions and values, and the development of practice under the best mentors. Teachers must be grounded in Indian values, languages, knowledge, ethos, and traditions while also being well-versed in the latest advances in education and pedagogy". The policy statement clearly indicates that the role and obligations of teacher education have substantially expanded in recent years. Concerns and expectations have increased because of national focus on qualitative learning outcomes. Teacher education also has to prepare teachers who mentor the young generation, encourage them to be competent, ready to work together and simultaneously remain competitive in the global context.

Teacher education these days is facing many challenges because of the specific mandate of 'education for all' and the constitutional provision of 'Right to Education'. It has to transform itself into a process that is practical in its approach, project and research based in its transactions, value based in its outlook and adopts 'learning to learn' as its motto. National Curriculum Framework for Teacher Education (NCFTE, 2009) mentions: "Teacher Education has to build the ability in the teacher to evolve one's knowledge to deal with different contexts, based on understanding and analysis of experience". In other words, teacher education is not a matter of simply acquiring degrees. It is more a matter of training and orienting the minds of young teachers towards understanding their pupils—their background, needs and interests. These motivated teachers will appreciate the societal faiths and values and provide a joyful learning environment conducive to a 'mind without fear'. The teacher must lead the child towards developing a creative and evidence-based thinking, adopting realistic and humanistic approach to social problems and a continued striving for excellence. Safety, security and due respect to the personal dignity of the child should receive utmost importance.

A good teacher raises the human soul from its egoistic state to the higher states of consciousness and thereby develops intensity of quest, concentration of mind and perseverance. A reflective teacher shuns arrogance and the sense of superiority. They have a deep faith in the natural capability of the pupil to learn. Great teachers always use error to arrive at truth, imperfection to arrive at perfection and awaken than instruct. They sow the seeds and observe them germinating under divine fostering. There is no imposition or passive acceptance on the part of the learners. An ideal teacher has a love for truth, a passion for justice and hatred for anything that ends in violence or human abuse. They have a feeling of fraternity towards students. However, to maintain the awe factor in students, they avoid intimate relationships.

Teaching being a profession, teacher education has to be a process of professional preparation of teachers. Professional preparation is an arduous task. It involves action on multiple fronts and from variety of perspectives. A profession is characterised by a sufficiently long period of rigorously planned and meticulously executed training. Young teachers have to acquire an organised body of knowledge on which the foundations of the undertaking are based. According to NEP 2020, this is possible only through a long duration and rigorous professional training in tandem with practical experience in the field, and a code of professional ethics that binds its members into a fraternity. The New Policy therefore stipulates that "All stand-alone TEIs will be required to convert to multidisciplinary institutions by 2025 and offer the 4-year integrated teacher preparation programme". It further mentions that teacher education must give due emphasis to developing reflective teachers with positive attitudes, values, and perspectives along with skills of the craft.

Teacher education has to be liberal, humanistic and responsive to the demands of inclusive education. Multidisciplinary education and teaching for diversity are the needs of contemporary times. "Teacher education needs to build capacities in the teacher to construct knowledge; to deal with different contexts, and to develop the abilities to discern and judge in moments of uncertainty and fluidity, characteristic of teaching-learning environments" (NCFTE, 2010).

Teacher education, as it is being practised in colleges of education today largely involves sermonising on idealistic lines. The curriculum transaction is mostly theoretical, bookish and hardly keeps in view the contemporary societal realities. The training of teachers and teacher educators is found utterly inadequate when it comes to the development of attitudes, values and human relationships. These affective outcomes require sustained positive learning environment and value-based interactions.

The process of present-day teacher education is skewed towards facts and information emanating from secondary sources. Practical and pragmatic aspects of present-day human enterprise are neither discussed nor experienced. The result is that the products of the system find the training received in the training colleges either utopian or not related to the realities and situations prevailing in the schools. In the emerging knowledge society, the content and process of teacher education have to strike a well-proportioned balance between theoretical and practical, technological and human inputs, global and local, modern and traditional, competition and cooperation, subjective and objective, as well as between philosophical, psychological and investigative.

One cannot deny the fact that teachers, in general, teach the way they have been taught in schools and colleges. Most of the pedagogical exhortations and verbalism hardly transform the teacher's approach and inclinations. It is time that the precepts and sermons are replaced by action and example. The teacher educators have to constantly remind themselves that teaching is not preaching, not simply training, not just communicating or indoctrinating, but it in fact involves developing an organic relationship between the teacher and the taught. Teaching has been beautifully described as the 'soul-to-soul exchange of ideas' between the teacher and the pupil.

We require a new generation of teachers, nay managers or facilitators, who can create a intellectually strong, creatively inclined and versatile workforce. Therefore, has rightly said, 'You cannot manufacture great teachers, but you can always manufacture great facilitators'. In the forthcoming knowledge age, a paradigm shift is required from the authoritarian one-way teaching to an active and participative learning and a democratic classroom learning ethos. Also, there is a need to re-examine the teacher education curriculum to humanise it in favour of human values, traditions and moral practices. Developing a feeling of compassion and empathy along with healthy and ethical relationship in the trainees may help in reducing and ultimately eliminating the inhuman activities and incidents in schools and colleges.

It is a matter of concern that instances of uncivilised behaviour of some unscrupulous teachers towards the young students are being reported in the media that vitiate the piety of the temples of knowledge. Providing humanistic and feeling-oriented teacher education has gained urgency because educated youths are taking the path of unsocial acts such as cheating, stealing and killing to acquire quick material gains. Teachers need to be duly sensitised towards these and many other contemporary social evils like child abuse, corporal punishment, bullying and sexual harassment. Teacher education, thus, is facing many challenges including safety and security of children. If we want to continue our march towards an enlightened and humane society, many more possibilities have to be explored to prepare teachers who can befittingly face challenges posed by the forces of moral degeneration due to modernisation, globalisation and consequent rising aspirations and material expectations.

Teaching is a human enterprise. It is the process of awakening souls by an awakened soul. Every child has the potential to grow and develop a teacher has to acknowledge this fact and convert it into action. This is to be accomplished by developing the children physically and intellectually and also by training their *Gyanendriya(s) and Karmendriya(s)* as well as their feelings and emotions. This process should lead to optimum and holistic development in a balanced manner. A teacher and their education and training programme must acknowledge the human endowments, needs and tendencies and thereby transform it accordingly. It is useful to remember the following:

Human beings are curious by nature. This active nature motivates them to investigate and learn. Therefore, the need is to provide them opportunities to:

- Explore, experiment and experience
- Discuss and ask questions
- Read, write, listen and express
- Think, reflect and improve

Teachers must use a variety of techniques/strategies to take care of diversity in a classroom:

- Lecture, lecture cum discussion, demonstration
- Group discussion and team games
- Opportunities for peer learning—exchange of information, ideas, views and experiences
- Giving assignments—before, in between and after

- Organising conferences/seminars, panel discussions
- Asking questions—leaving some questions unanswered
- Field trip and visits
- Use of information and communication Technology (ICT), presentations by students, internet surfing, Referring to websites/portals/CDs/online resources
- Team teaching, giving handouts
- Brainstorming sessions
- Global conferences, international exchanges, webinars, etc.

Sensitise teachers towards specific aptitudes of both boys and girls. Each should be given appropriate additional educational inputs in supplement to the core curriculum to optimise their specific talents and innate capabilities. In this context, NEP 2020 has also emphasised that "Teachers will aim to encourage students with singular interests and/or talents in the classroom by giving them supplementary enrichment material and guidance and encouragement".

Any future teacher education curriculum should address the following feeling-related realistic issues:

1. **Every human being has expectations and aspirations:** A specific deficiency related to aspiration level is often observed particularly in students coming from poorer economic backgrounds and those from rural areas in our country. Teacher educators in training colleges and teachers in general education institutions should strive to raise the quality of aspiration of such students so that they aim high and act towards that direction.
2. **Courage and perseverance are two important qualities of a human being:** Our present-day curriculum lacks the components of courage, bravery and the quality of perseverance, which are so important for citizens and their success in life. Situations, activities and conscious efforts are needed at the teacher education level to instill these in young boys and girls. True teachers value and develop in students the 'courage to speak

the truth', 'to reward the right and punish the wrong', 'to save the weak and those in distress', 'to persevere in the face of adversities' and 'to raise voice against social evils'. These, and many other social and child-related issues, need to be underlined in the curriculum. The country today, more than any other time, requires such role models for the young. NCC, scouting, NSS, adventure sports, disaster management, the campaign against child abuse and sex discrimination, preventive measures towards health issues and safety and security-related issues need to be emphasised in teacher education colleges.

3. ***Purusharthas,* namely *Dharma, Arth, Kama* and *Moksha,* are relevant goals for living a wholesome life:** Education must stress on the essence of life on earth. These are some goals in life to be accomplished by everyone. Student–teachers should to be told that there is no scope for helplessness, suicidal tendency or depression. Spiritual development, meditation, environmental awareness, etc., must form an integral component of teacher education. A unique curriculum of yoga needs to be devised by expert groups, especially meant for teacher education, to enhance healthful life, improve power of concentration, power of judgment decision making. Mind training, silence, *chintan, manan* and reflection are some more elements to aspire for in this context.
4. **Sensitising Human and Child Rights:** Fundamental rights and fundamental duties enshrined in the Constitution, human rights as per UN Charter, child rights and related content are necessary today for teacher education, especially in the face of child abuse, sexual assault, corporal punishment and cruelty by a section of teachers. There is need to reaffirm faith in fundamental human rights and the dignity and worth of human beings.
5. **Education for Peace and Harmony:** Today constant threats are being posed due to intolerance, fanaticism,

dispute and discordance. Taste for violence and its escalating trend require reflective engagement with meaningful aspects of living. There is a need to consciously counter the negative influence of increasing violence. Non-violent conflict resolution skills, negotiation skills and social justice should be woven into the teacher education curriculum.

6. **Education for Sustainable Development:** Sustainable development is one that satisfies society's needs without diminishing the prospects of future generations. Today economy and ecology are becoming ever more interwoven and hence education for sustainable development rightfully should find a place in teacher education curriculum.

The foregoing discussion clearly indicates that there is a need to re-examine the teacher education curriculum. It requires to be humanised to obviate the pressures of inhuman activities and incidents. Gandhiji's seven sins can form a perfect reference point for reorienting the teacher education curriculum. These social sins are 'wealth without work, education without character, science without humanity, commerce without morality, politics without principles, pleasure without conscience and worship without sacrifice'.

References

GOI, MHRD. National Education Policy, 2020,15.4, page 40, New Delhi.

National Curriculum Framework for Teacher Education. (2009) National Council for Teacher Education (NCTE), New Delhi.

National Curriculum Framework for Teacher Education (NCFTE) (2010) National Council for Teacher Education (NCTE), New Delhi.

13

Reimagining Teacher Education

The behaviour of a teacher within a school system has to be compatible with the contemporary philosophy of education. It has to be in line with the changing needs and requirements of the schools, communities and the learning needs of present-day learners. Instead of dealing with mere generalities, teacher education should emphasise imparting specific skills through doing rather than simply telling and sermonising. Objectives of teacher education must take into cognizance the societal, professional, technological and ethical needs of twenty-first century teachers. In the midst of sweeping changes in the societal and technological front followed by the explosion of knowledge and complexities of modern life, there is a need to reimagine and accordingly redesign the teacher education programmes—both pre-service and in-service.

Education and training of teachers have always been a matter of concern to national planners and policymakers. Efforts in this direction in the post-independent India took concrete shape when the National Council of Educational Research and Training (NCERT) was formed in 1961, and simultaneously, four Regional Colleges of Education were started in four regions of the country. Teacher education programmes of varied durations and different specialisations were introduced and experimented upon. Department of Teacher Education in the National Institute of Education, in collaboration with various other content departments, came out with model curricula for teacher education. This was followed by a revision of curricula by different university departments of education. Later, a need was felt for a regulatory body for teacher education. To give it teeth, it was ultimately established as a separate body through a Parliamentary Act.

During that period, universities floated correspondence courses in teacher education that unfortunately degenerated into money-spinning propositions, thus, for the first time, putting a question mark on the quality of teacher education. With the establishment of the National Council for Teacher Education (NCTE), first drastic step taken by it was to close down these correspondence courses, especially for B.Ed. By any standard, it was considered a welcome decision on the way to reforming teacher education. But as the later developments indicate, the reform remained short-lived since the system had to face serious distortions in the form of a phenomenon of 'non-attending students', 'non-attending faculty' and even 'non-existing colleges'. The pertinent question that remains to be answered is 'while a number of parallel bodies like NCTE and NAAC at the Centre, Universities and Directorates of Higher Education in the States are said to be continuously monitoring the teacher education institutions, how and why such a situation arose and is persisting in some States?' The answer probably lies in the fact that 'It is easy to abandon a programme, but it is difficult to redesign it by taking lessons from the past'. As Sri Aurobindo maintains, "...past is indeed a huge force of conservation, but of conservation that is not immobile, that on the contrary offers itself as material for change and a new realisation that the present is the constant change and new actual realisation which the past desires and compels; and that the future is that force".

The roots of this malice can be found in the bureaucratic decision-making process. As already discussed elsewhere, when correspondence courses were closed down, the decision was not backed by any systematic study of the clientele of these courses. No serious attention was given to questions such as 'Who were going for correspondence courses? What was their motivation? Why do they not prefer a regular course?' Any such study would have zeroed in on a number of socio-economic and cultural factors behind this compulsion. Based on the results of a fact-finding study, a high-level committee of experts could have gone deeper into the problem and suggested an alternative strategy having better effectiveness and transparency. This never happened.

The regulatory bodies which were supposed to fight such distortions basically started working on preparing norms for classrooms, faculty, resource rooms, playgrounds, etc. Later the designated inspection committees, in the name of adherence to set norms by an institution, started arm-twisting techniques for petty gains. These rigidities went to the extent of physically measuring even the resource rooms and conference rooms up to the last centimetre using measuring tapes. In this context, it is worthwhile to mention that infrastructural facilities, as many studies have revealed, in themselves do not help in enhancing the quality of instruction. But as of today, all inspection committees just check the infrastructural norms as per their whims, making the whole process bureaucratic, mechanical and, at times, ridiculous. Thus, the very purpose of inspection is defeated.

Alas! No inspection committee ever went into the classroom, never inspected the teaching-learning process, nor did they go into the quality of activities like assignments, term papers, tests, innovations or co-curricular activities. They never went to the playground and witnessed games and sports in action. In such a set-up where the intention is fault finding, putting stumbling blocks and using the platform for corrupt practices, genuine teacher education and institutions striving to attain quality suffered silently. They had nowhere to go for redressing their grievances as even those at the helm of affairs who do understand the importance of academic aspect conveniently succumbed to the 'system' in which any quick or positive decision was seen with suspicion. Delay and harassment ultimately led to decaying of such well-meaning institutions. They had no other alternative but to follow the rut.

The NEP, 2020 in this context, quoting Justice Verma Commission, mentions, "The Justice J. S. Verma Commission

(2012) constituted by the Supreme Court has stated that a majority of stand-alone teaching institutes—over 10,000 in number—are not even attempting serious teacher education, but are essentially selling degrees for a price. The regulatory efforts so far have neither been able to curb the corruption rampant in the system nor enforce basic standards for quality and, in fact, have had the negative effect of curbing the growth of excellence and innovation in the sector. The sector and its regulatory system are therefore in urgent need of revitalisation through radical action, in order to raise standards and restore integrity, credibility, efficacy and high quality to the teacher education system".

Let us take as another example, the case of a two-year B.Ed.—a well-intended reform put forward by NCTE to raise the academic standards of teacher education institutions. But even after a decade of its experimentation in regional institutes of education under NCERT, it could not be implemented in the country till it was ultimately enforced by legal provisions. Among private players, those who had political clout or money power were thriving while honest and meek managements managing institutions for their passion for service were silently suffering. Each reform brings along with it newer corrupt practices. The need is to clearly define and distinguish the role of each regulatory body. Let decision of one body be respected by another body.

It is time that an environment of trust is created among government and private institutions. A distinction must be made between those private institutions that are sincere and those that are unscrupulous. Grant-in-aid to promising self-financing teacher education institutions can go a long way in this endeavour. Similar discrimination prevails when it comes to the training of teachers, teacher educators and educational administrators. While adequate in-service training facilities are available for schools and colleges in the government sector, there is hardly any such facility for private and self-financing institutions. Hence, either a separate body is created or some good private or self-financing teacher education institution is selected for offering in-service training of teachers and teacher educators working in private and self-financing schools and colleges. Affiliating to a Board or university may initiate steps to create such a mechanism in collaboration with the institutions by providing incentives to promising institutions to work as the nodal agency.

Further, every teacher education institution should compulsorily be asked to adopt one neighbourhood school and provide it academic, training and research support. Even training of pre-service and in-service teachers needs to be streamlined for every stage of education, right from ECCE to higher secondary and even post-secondary. This should be done in a coherent and systematic manner under one umbrella instead of in a fragmented manner as at present. This would mean composite teacher education institutions offering training of teachers for all stages of education, right from pre-primary to higher secondary and beyond.

Teacher Education in Today's Perspective

"The tasks of teachers today are more complex and demanding than in the past. They have to respond to the wishes of parents regarding educational outcomes, the social need for wider access to education and pressures for democratic participation within the schools". (OECD Report 1990). There was a time when the teacher was considered good if they made prior preparations for the lecture, used teaching aids while explaining and taught as per their meticulously written notes. Today the parents are not ready to accept a teacher simply because they are active, works hard to prepare their lectures and deliver emphatically the same in a classroom situation. Their main contention today is 'if the student hasn't learnt, the teacher hasn't taught'. The value of teaching gets its legitimacy only if learning takes place on the part of the child. This calls for activity and simultaneous involvement of the child in the process of learning. Teaching and learning cannot be separated any longer. The role of the teacher is to facilitate the process of learning by skilful resource management, mutual active involvement and testing the status of learning at every stage.

Need for Specialised Programmes

Today need is also being felt for specialised teacher education programmes for senior secondary stage, vocational education and training, computer education, engineering education and management education. There is, therefore, a need to have a comprehensive policy of teacher education in the country. The university system should come forward with new models of teacher education to meet the newer avenues being generated by the knowledge society of tomorrow. Teacher education system today must face questions like: 'Are we preparing our children for coping with the newer opportunities in the booming service sector?' 'Do we organise SMART classes to create curious minds and thereby develop productive, analytic and creative democratic citizens of tomorrow?' 'Are we laying enough emphasis on developing critical and creative thinking?' 'How will the system develop twenty-first century skills in the student population?' and so on.

The nation at present is moving ahead, crossing the information age and entering the knowledge age. As implied in the Report of the National Knowledge Commission, one finds a dramatic change in the nature of the world of work in near future. Manual and mechanical jobs are giving way to thinking and knowledge jobs. The National Education Policy 2020, too, has expressed similar concerns. It states, "The world is undergoing rapid changes in the knowledge landscape. With the rise of big data, machine learning and artificial intelligence, many unskilled jobs worldwide may be taken over by machines, while the need for skilled labour, particularly involving mathematics, computer science and data science, in conjunction with multi-disciplinary abilities across the sciences, social sciences and humanities, will be in rapidly increasing demand". Youngsters, therefore, will have to be trained for new types of opportunities in jobs like medical transcription, call centre jobs, jobs related to cyber cafe, e-learning, e-business, multimedia packaging, computerised photography, video conferencing, mobile technology, event management, resorts, spa & parlour management, jobs in entertainment and music industry, sports industry, health and fashion industry, food and nutrition industry, hospitality industry, telecommunication industry, institutional housekeeping, interior decoration, nursery growing, floriculture, tissue culture, education and training services and in many such other emerging areas.

Obviously, we would require competent teachers who can provide education and training in these emerging fields to develop employable skills among future citizens. It is high time that vocational teacher education emerges as a distinct field of teacher education in the country. Skill development, skill up-gradation and a multi-skilling outlook, are essential to keep a competitive edge in the global market.

Professional Preparation of Teachers

It is an open secret that present-day teacher training system is the weakest link mainly because of quantitative expansion and its predominantly theoretical orientation. Teaching is a profession. Therefore, teacher education has to be a process of professional preparation of teachers. Professional preparation is an arduous task. It involves action on multiple fronts and from variety of perspectives. A profession is characterised by a sufficiently long period of education and training, involving both theory and practice. Professional teachers have to acquire an organised body of knowledge on which the foundations and pedagogical processes of education are based. This is possible through an appropriate duration of formal and rigorous professional training in tandem with practical experience in the field and a code of professional ethics that binds its members into a fraternity.

Incidentally, NEP 2020 took a close look at teacher education and rightly suggested that "In order to improve and reach the levels of integrity and credibility required to restore the prestige of the teaching profession and thereby attain a successful school system, the Regulatory system shall be empowered to phase out substandard and dysfunctional Teacher Education Institutions (TEI) that do not meet basic educational criteria. All TEIs will be held accountable to adherence to the basic criteria for approval of their programmes; after giving one year for remedy, if any breaches are found, they will be shut down if the breaches are not remedied". The policy document emphatically stated that "The teacher education must be conducted within composite multidisciplinary institutions having, apart from education, departments of psychology, philosophy, sociology, neuroscience, Indian languages, arts, history, and literature, as well as various other specialised subjects such as science and mathematics etc. All stand-alone TEIs will be required to convert to multidisciplinary institutions by 2025 and offer the 4-year integrated teacher preparation programme. All large multidisciplinary universities—including all public universities as well as all Model Multidisciplinary Colleges shall establish, develop and house outstanding education departments which, aside from carrying out cutting-edge research in various aspects of education, will also run B.Ed. Programmes to educate future teachers". As per the policy, "The 4-year integrated B.Ed. offered by such multidisciplinary HEIs will, by 2030, become the minimal degree qualification for school teachers".

It may be noted that the policy made an important statement, almost path-breaking, when it said, "Each HEI offering the 4-year integrated B.Ed. may also design a 2-year B.Ed. on its campus for outstanding students who have already received a bachelor's degree in a specialised subject and wish to pursue teaching". It may be hoped that with the new incarnation, teacher education may go to develop reflective teachers having a positive attitude, desirable human values and futuristic perspectives along with skills of craft of teaching.

Need for Innovation and Experimentation

Teacher education has to be liberal, humanistic and responsive to the demands of inclusive education. Multicultural education and teaching for diversity are the needs of contemporary times. It has to be futuristic and should build capacities in the teacher to help the child to construct knowledge, deal with emerging new contexts and discern and judge in the moments of uncertainty. Therefore, it is time that some innovative ideas are considered and experiments are conducted to make the system more effective and efficient.

For example, can we think in terms of developing a cadre of rural teachers? Just as Navodaya Vidyalayas have been created for nurturing rural talents, on similar lines, rural teacher education colleges can be created and housed in rural areas with content cum methodology courses that are suitable to rural needs and specialisations. These colleges will attract rural talents to the teaching profession and can be affiliated to the rural universities. The trainees being from rural areas, will be well conversant with rural ethos, needs and limitations. They will not only stay in rural areas but also slowly develop into a cadre of teachers based in rural areas having specialised knowledge of rural adolescents.

Conclusion

Teacher education is facing many challenges due to contemporary socio-economic and political compulsions. If we want to continue our march towards an enlightened and humane society, many more possibilities have to be explored to prepare teachers who can befittingly face challenges posed by the forces of modernisation, globalisation and consequent rising aspirations. Seeing the teacher as a dispenser of information and the child as the storehouse of information is unacceptable in today's perspective. The teacher can no longer continue to transfer the accumulated information through lectures or by reading from textbooks. Transformation of a teacher into a facilitator, making them conversant with online resources and preparing them for the digital age technology cannot be overemphasised in today's perspective.

References

GOI, MHRD. National Education Policy, 2020, 15.2, page 40, New Delhi.

OECD (1990) Education 1960-1990 The OECD Perspective. OECD, Paris.

GOI, MHRD. National Education Policy 2020, 0.2, page 3, New Delhi.

14
Developing Research Culture

Doing research is intellectually refreshing and mentally stimulating. It is good for one's career. Research establishes and improves institutional reputation and plays a crucial role in faculty advancement towards higher career path. Undertaking research proves to be a satisfying experience to the enquiring mind. Research helps to break away from the routine. It not only satiates the curiosity but also challenges the thinking faculties. It instils a desire to improve one's own experience. Results of research have been found useful in decision-making, monitoring, evaluating and administering. Research-based interventions have gone to improve the teaching-learning processes. The person involved in research finds the process interesting since it provides an opportunity to probe in-depth and allows to explore diverse possibilities. Individuals also enjoy discovering new ideas by resorting to new ways of interpretation. As said earlier, a researcher not only develops professionally but also gets recognition, ultimately leading to better career prospects. Thus, research not only enriches the individual and helps in improving practices but also enriches and refreshes the teaching, and even enhances the reputation of an institution.

Teaching and research have a generic relationship. Each enriches and gives impetus to the other. An institution preparing teachers and teacher educators, therefore, must develop a culture centred on research and innovation. This entails that faculty and students will have to inculcate the necessary skills and capabilities to appreciate and conduct research activities. At the same time, it requires the right type of leadership along with provision of adequate administrative support in terms of funding, incentives, equipment, training, scholarship and facilities for publication and dissemination.

If we want student-teachers to be research oriented, we have to ensure that the teacher educators themselves engage in research and innovation activities and take up worthwhile research projects, individually and collectively. However, for this to take shape, the first prerequisite is to create a positive research culture within the institution and among the faculty members. It would mean creating awareness about research and innovation for solving practical problems faced in teaching-learning. The habit of cooperative functioning in a group, providing necessary support or incentive, encouragement from top management and other positive steps to generate an urge for doing research or taking up innovative practices would go a long way towards developing a research culture.

A culture of research would imply providing a supportive context wherein research is demystified, research ideas are freely discussed and research/development projects are undertaken and valued. It is essential that in an institutional setup, everyone is expected and given opportunities to contribute in creating an atmosphere conducive to research. Creating a research culture is a long-drawn process. A positive research culture and support to individual researchers will provide necessary impetus in leading the faculty members towards worthwhile and significant research activities. A strong research culture is an outcome of willing involvement of the faculty in research activities that may be as simple as preparing a review of a research article or as rigorous as undertaking an independent research project.

Following are some more ideas to create a research culture across the organisation:

1. Facilitating open discussion in a collaborative environment wherein research ideas and proposals leading to innovative practices are presented and finalised. Faculty members accept and take up such activities willingly in a cooperative framework.

2. Opportunities for presentations, seminars, workshops, panel discussions on improving research culture, showcasing individual or departmental achievements.
3. Encouraging writing, publishing and bringing out booklets, magazines, souvenirs and pamphlets on education
4. Having brainstorming sessions to generate research/ innovative ideas
5. Making available research literature, research journals and incentives for encouraging publication and dissemination
6. Providing seed money
7. Bringing out a research journal

Need for Motivation

Teacher education institutions in a democracy have a special role to play in producing teachers and teacher educators who are competent, committed, flexible and ready to modify and improve based on new research evidence. Every teaching institution requires a research culture of its own to keep on taking fresh initiatives and generating new ideas. It is only through continuous research and innovation that teachers enliven their professional life, and the system gets much-needed new inputs and directions to remain vibrant and dynamic.

Unfortunately, an average teacher educator these days feels that research is not his cup of tea. It is meant for a few who have a knack for it. To them research is too serious an exercise to be attempted by everyone. Young teacher educators generally shun research largely because they lack practical research experience. They do not feel confident to take up research studies. Most of the time, they do not know how and where to start. Even they cannot see the benefits of research and innovation in the absence of due support from colleagues and management. Experience, however, shows that resistance to engaging in research at times melts away when it is combined with a research project directly related to a professional development initiative like registering for a Ph.D.

Fortunately, teacher educators are recruited with Post Graduate degree in education and hence are aware of the various dimensions of educational research. Probably due to the largely theoretical orientation of their training, they are not well-versed in practice. This leads to lack of self-confidence. Therefore, to them, the concept of research in institutional context needs to be properly clarified, and they should be trained in essential research skills. Nothing is more effective at this stage than peer learning in a cooperative setup. This idea probably brings in the need for a group of like-minded, motivated colleagues who have an urge to move away from the tangent. Opportunities for sharing experiences, offering quality interactions, constant mentoring and positive reinforcements enable them to come out of their shells and begin trying something new or different. This would, however, require positive group dynamics and effective leadership within the group to ensure productive functioning of the group. Academic guidance by the Principal and clear direction by a senior colleague with full backing from the management can galvanise the group for action.

Teacher educators, in general, and group members, in particular, should be made to appreciate that they are capable of initiating simple innovations involving students. To begin with, they may conduct community surveys, take up action research projects to modify existing practices leading to better learning on the part of students or prepare case studies. Gradually they can introduce precision and rigour by using qualitative and quantitative research methodologies. In-depth research on major aspects can be attempted by a group of research-oriented educators by way of independent researches, multicentric researches or sponsored researches. Today when emphasis has shifted from teaching to learning, knowledge construction in place of passive receiving, stress on stimulation of sense perceptions through ICT techniques and focus on participatory classroom ethos, every dynamic institution requires creative solutions to traditional problems by resorting to research-based interventions.

Research and Innovation Forum

It is in this context that, based on actual experience, the author proposes the creation of a cell in every teacher education institution. It will be composed of faculty members willing to initiate research and innovation activities for individual professional satisfaction as well as to bring novelty in teaching -learning and institutional planning. The cell can be suitably named as 'Educational Research Associates', or 'Research Management Cell' or simply 'Research and Innovation Forum'. However, efforts should be made to enlarge this cell gradually over a period of time to include more and more members, ultimately covering the total cohort. An experiment conducted in this respect indicates that it requires a lot of persuasion through success stories before additional members join the group. This mechanism of forming a group will help in building a research team within the institution. The team members will be able to take advantage of others' expertise, sharing their own experiences and thus learn together. Individuals need to be encouraged and given a free hand to pursue their own ideas for innovative projects. However, constructive guidance and direction will help in concretising the projects or activities. It is advisable to encourage interdepartmental and collaborative projects. Conducting frequent workshops on identifying and defining research questions, techniques of data collection, analysis, interpretation and writing up of the report, will further facilitate the task of the group members.

Constitution of the Cell/ Forum

1. A group of willing faculty members (5–8 or 10) to begin with, interested in generating new ideas and novel ways of doing
2. A faculty member with vision and research ideas to initiate and coordinate the activities of the group
3. The Principal, Vice Principal or an active researcher may serve as a patron to the group
4. Gradually enlarging the group as others get interested.

Activities

The activities of the Cell will be specifically geared to:

1. Developing interest in reading, writing and listening about research-related literature, practices, projects and reports
2. Providing hands-on experience in writing innovative, creative research articles
3. Preparing executive summaries and abstracts of research articles and reports
4. Taking up action research projects. Incidentally, many action research projects are of low cost
5. Involving students in innovative activities and projects
6. Publication of articles and research papers
7. Making research proposals and seeking external funding
8. Conducting seminars and conferences
9. Preparing and publishing book reviews
10. Presentations of their work by researchers and discussion within the group
11. Presentations by group members on topics of mutual interest
12. Bringing out a newsletter for dissemination of research results
13. Developing a research corner in the library by collecting research literature, journals, dissertations, theses, etc

These are only some suggestive activities and not exhaustive in any way. The group can function smoothly if the management provides some seed money and allows recurring expenses. The group may meet during lunch hour or after college hours. Each member, after thorough discussion, may take up one or the other activity from the following to start with:

a) Reading a published research article, writing its abstract and presenting it to the group for discussion
b) Inviting research scholars to present their work and hold discussions with a focus on further research ideas
c) Taking up small innovative projects in one's specialised area with active participation of students

d) Writing articles, making reports, preparing summaries of project reports, preparing reviews, writing books and so on

e) Participating in writing competitions at district, state, or national level as and when these are announced

f) Producing formal research proposals along with financial implications and time budgeting for external funding

Such simple writing presenting and listening exercises will help to prepare the members for more rigorous exercises later. This may then be followed by identifying, finalising and undertaking action research projects related to teaching -learning, improving institutional functioning or developing specific abilities in students. After they successfully complete an action research project and report its outcomes, they will feel better prepared to take up applied research projects either individually or collectively. Such a gradual process will ease resistance to new ideas and ensure wider participation by other faculty members, thus establishing an ethos in favour of research and innovation in a teacher education institution.

Conclusion

The preceding description emphatically brings out the fact that engaging in research activities brings in fresh air to breathe, thereby providing fresh oxygen to every part of the institutional body. Teachers being change agents, can bring positive change in the functioning of the institution, improve upon their teaching quality, inculcate right attitudes and values in students and raise the effectiveness of management by conducting experiments, initiating group activities, using modern educational technology and collecting and introducing new methods and ideas through research-based interventions. Teacher educators, therefore, have a special responsibility to empower the pupil teachers to make them capable of doing worthwhile research to strengthen teaching and learning in their respective schools. 'Example is better than precept', and hence initiation of research culture in teacher education institutions will hopefully get transferred to schools through the medium of research-oriented pupil teachers.

15

Effectiveness of In-service Teacher Training

In the field of in-service teacher education as well, the situation is not very rosy. Driven by the need for continuous training and retraining, it has become almost customary to organise orientation or refresher courses for teachers and teacher educators with a view to coaxing and cajoling the kingpin for better performance. An in-service training or orientation programme can have a lasting impact only if parallel and simultaneous inputs are provided, such as provision of desired infrastructural facilities, readiness for curriculum reform, efficient systemic management, use of latest educational technology and due recognition of teacher's status. Opportunities for professional growth and a helping and innovative institutional ethos are other requirements for bringing out the best in a person as a teacher. In other words, teachers and their performance have to be seen in a total institutional perspective and dealt accordingly.

Parental aspirations and rising social expectations, along with rapid changes in technology leading to virtual classrooms and e-learning resources, have put tremendous pressure on contemporary school education. Consequent revamping and reorientation of school curriculum have led the content and process of school education into a state of flux. Amidst this fluid situation in school curriculum, understandably, the content and process of teacher education too cannot remain static. It is no secret that the pre-service degree of BEd is under severe criticism both in terms of its quality and effectiveness. This criticism becomes more serious and real when the trainees passing out of the teacher training colleges themselves fail to justify the effectiveness, utility and transferability of their teacher training in their day-to-day teaching because of many academic and administrative factors. The school, its classrooms and even its total ethos are experiencing tremendous change both qualitatively and quantitatively. More often than not, these trainees privately confess that as a matter of routine, they are compelled to discard all soft pedagogy taught in a training college right outside the classroom since, in the realistic framework, they are compelled to comply with the given instructions. They find the regimented school environment a totally different world altogether, wherein the idealistic axioms of philosophy and sociology largely prove to be misplaced. These new teachers soon fall into the rut and find no time or chance to practice the pedagogy taught to them during their training period. They neither find the time nor feel the necessity to use different methodologies for the content to be taught and in line with the needs of the students. In other words, under the pressure of workload, a large number of students per class, and result (marks) oriented parents and school administration, they slowly but surely get moulded in the prevailing traditional groove of chalk, talk and stick. However, a few exceptions cannot be ruled out either. Thus, in such a regimented school set-up, the degree of BEd remains nothing but a mere license to enter the profession.

The teacher training programmes, refresher courses and faculty development programmes being run as part of in-service training of teachers, also suffer from similar lacunae. Conducting such programmes by some specialised institutions has become almost a routine. In these programmes, selected resource persons deliver pre-prepared lectures with the pious intention of motivating the kingpin to improve their teaching. In the absence of any systematic impact study of these refresher or training programmes, it is difficult to say how far these programmes are fulfilling the stated objectives. Or to what extent these outcomes are getting translated into better and improved teaching-learning in schools. Also, in this context, we often fail to realise that a teacher in a school does not function in isolation. They are part of a bigger system. In order to bring in any improvement in this system, inputs have to be planned at every point in a harmonious and coordinated fashion by giving due weightage to every element within the sub-system. This is because each element in the sub-system is organically linked. Any improvement in one would require concomitant upgrading of others. Therefore, any attempt to develop a single element, however significant it may be, without simultaneous improvement of others will result in some cosmetic behavioural changes that will prove to be peripheral and superficial. Such changes are neither implementable in the absence of necessary conditions nor sustainable. As said earlier, sustainability can be ensured only by paying due attention to every element for simultaneous and coordinated development. In the present case, there is a lurking fear that in spite of best intentions, the urge to change may even lead to cynicism amongst the participants.

The point under discussion may get further clarified by taking pre-service and in-service programmes together as a sub-system of the total school education. The teacher being an element of the sub-system is no doubt important, but their role, functioning and efficiency are dependent on many other systemic factors such as congenial teaching and learning environment an understanding, encouraging and forward-looking administration availability and accessibility to a variety of technological and other resources, opportunities for innovation and professional growth and a helping and supportive institutional ethos in favour of experimentation and innovation. Good service conditions, residential accommodation, facilities for physical and cultural development, recreation, etc., are other important and useful requirements for bringing out the best in a person as a teacher.

In other words, the teacher and his performance have to be seen in a total physical, social and emotional perspective and dealt accordingly. Merely making a teacher go through a ritual periodically by attending, most of the time, ill-conceived and hurriedly organised training programmes, at best tends to raise the aspiration level of the teacher and perhaps their enthusiasm to perform better. But the zeal thus created, in the absence of supporting and encouraging a holistic environment within the school, proves to be short-lived. Dull and drab routine of the school, result-oriented outlook of the administration and examination oriented curriculum deny the learners to derive personal satisfaction by engaging in critical thinking and creative manipulations. Apathy of the administration towards financial and other commitments, lack of required infrastructure and emphasis on covering syllabus disallows an enthusiastic change-oriented teacher from trying anything different, new or innovative. The layer of enthusiasm that an occasional training programme adds is hardly able to change the ground situation. More often than not, the layer fades away in the face of rigid bureaucratic rules and regulations that hardly give any freedom for experimentation and innovation.

In view of the above, any attempt to bring in reform that is genuine and well-intended must address the system in a holistic manner instead of tinkering with isolated elements here and there. The need is to simultaneously energise all the elements of each sub-system. Any shortcut strategy is bound to result in wastage of precious time and resources. Often populist methods like massive training programmes covering few days instead of achieving the stated objectives, tend to breed skepticism and even frustration within the system.

The school system too requires developing a positive and pro-change mindset. In a positive school ethos, channels of communication at different levels remain open within a broad institutional framework. In such a school, an open mindset prevails wherein changes can be tried, new ideas can be introduced, and learning environment conducive to exploration and experimentation can be established. In such a school, 'covering' the course and 'manipulating' the results give way to self-directed experiential learning on the part of the students and student-centric reflective teaching on the part of the teacher.

Sincere efforts are essential to make the process of reform or improvement sustainable. This is possible only when each element of the sub-system gets nourishment—timely and systematically, by introducing necessary systemic reforms such that the total system organically grows like we notice in stem, leaves and branches of a healthy tree. To make it more explicit, teacher training programmes can have desirable and lasting impact only when parallel and simultaneous inputs are provided to related elements within the sub-system, such as provision of quality infrastructure, enriched and varied curriculum inputs, efficient and farsighted management, provision of latest communication technology and due encouragement and recognition to enthusiastic teachers. Any effort to introduce change in a piecemeal manner will only breed dissatisfaction and frustration.

Conclusion

It is time that a comprehensive review is undertaken of the way training programmes are organised. Special attention needs to be paid to those training programmes that are, most of the time, conducted just to complete the formalities or requirements of a particular scheme. The discussion in this chapter makes it amply clear that to have the desired impact of these programmes on the system, it would be necessary to take a holistic view of the systemic needs, including training, which will, of course, form an important part. The teacher has to be freed from many rigid and obsolete rules and regulations, financial constraints as well as the whims and fancies of administrators so that they can try new ideas and innovations to bring in modifications or changes as a follow-up of the training programmes. Each element of every sub-system should receive timely intervention and due attention, and the required enrichment or modification, even by relaxing rules if need be.

Section 3
Vocational Education and Training

16

Vocational Education and Training: An Indian Perspective

Introduction

Individuals, enterprises, the economy and the society as a whole benefit from human resource development. With promising potential for continuous development of competent and skilled manpower, the economy firmly moves forward and becomes productive, innovative and competitive. Even the fundamental human values of equality, equity, social justice, gender equality, non-discrimination, social responsibility and participatory democracy get strengthened when youths of the nation become self-sufficient and self-dependent by proper skill education and training. With the knowledge age overtaking the Information Age, complete world of work is getting transformed because of the rapid and multidimensional technological changes. These changes can be seen and felt in new management practices, new forms of business organisation, emergence of global markets for products and services, international competition, online education and emergence and thriving of multinational companies.

These developments undoubtedly pose challenges to job seekers and those going for entrepreneurial ventures. However, at the same time, these offer tremendous opportunities to the young generation. Such developments are increasing the need for application of human knowledge and skills to economic activities. Development of flexible, employable and quality-conscious human resources through vocational education and training (VET) has become an imperative to take advantage of the opportunities and also to face the challenges coming in the way.

Education must ensure optimum development of the human personality and citizenship qualities. Elementary education should lay foundation for employability by providing general core work skills, work habits and work ethics. At the higher stages, occupational knowledge and industry-based professional competencies should be developed to facilitate the transition into the contemporary world of work. This must be followed by lifelong and continuing education such that an individual's skills and competencies are maintained and successively improved as work, technology and skill requirements change.

VET is required not only to improve the overall socio-economic conditions but also to prevent and combat social exclusion and discrimination. Keeping in view the present-day realities, education cannot be separated from training. Elementary and secondary education thus provides the foundation on which an effective VET system should be built.

Emergence of the Need

The emergence of the need for a VET system, especially in post-independent India, can be attributed to the problems and issues being faced by the educational world as well as by the occupational world. These have arisen mainly because of the rising aspirations of people, large number of educated unemployed, dearth of middle-level manpower in the industrial and post-industrial era and the expanding vocational world due to globalisation, liberalisation and privatisation. With the advent of information and communication technology (ICT) and in keeping with the requirements of the fast-approaching knowledge age, a strong need has been generated to introduce vocational and practical training elements into the purely bookish and theoretical school curriculum.

The prevailing school curriculum is not in accordance with the interest, abilities and aptitudes of students. This is resulting in a large percentage of dropouts or pushouts from the system. Most of the students prefer to go aimlessly for higher education, thus creating undue pressure on the tertiary education system and its quality. Strong impetus on universalisation of elementary education has led to the expansion of the secondary education system. Students from all sections of the society are joining the school today. A hiatus between needs of the economy and school curriculum is clearly visible.

Employers find the products of the system unemployable because of their purely academic orientation. Girls today are joining schools in big numbers. There is a need for non-traditional and technology-oriented courses to accommodate their talents. All these developments led to the demand for need-based vocational courses to suit diverse clientele in the rural sector, urban sector, unorganised sector and those from the weaker sections of the society. VET has, therefore, to accommodate the needs of diverse target groups, including disadvantaged groups, women, persons with special needs, rural and tribal students and people with disabilities, older workers, the long-term unemployed, low-skilled workers, migrant workers and workers laid off due to economic reform programmes. Non-formal, flexible and need-based VET programmes will have to be offered to neo-literates, unemployed youths, school dropouts and partially employed persons.

Vocational Education and Training in Indian Perspective

VET subsumes itself within the holistic concept of human resource development. One of the important aims of education is to prepare a person to be self-reliant. In the contemporary world, it implies providing practical education for life and livelihood. With the growing pace of economic development, much emphasis is being given globally to vocational, technical and professional education. It is generally agreed that knowledge gained must be functional and applicable in solving problems faced by the individual and the society. Vocational education and training ET in this context is education in the broader sense of the term. In other words, liberal education emphasising intellectual, moral, and socio-emotional development, and vocational education aiming at economic and industrial progress are complementary to each other. VET thus incorporates the meaning given to vocational education with sharp focus on the development of skills through specialised training for enhanced employability.

This thinking has been succinctly reflected in the National Policy on Education (1986), which considered the introduction of systematic, well-planned and rigorously implemented programme of vocational education to be crucial in the proposed educational reorganisation. As stated in the policy, it intends to prepare students for identified occupations spanning several areas of activity to be ordinarily provided after the secondary stage. Emphasis will also be on development of attitudes, knowledge and skills for entrepreneurship and self-employment. The objectives specified in the policy for VET are to (a) provide diversification of educational opportunities to enhance individual employability, (b) reduce the mismatch between demand and supply of skilled manpower and (c) provide an alternative for those pursuing higher education without particular interest or purpose. In keeping with this stipulation, VET has been conceptualised at the national level to enable students to choose subjects and programmes in a wide field of knowledge and skills as per their aptitude, interests, and abilities. Vocational education and training are expected to improve their occupational competence in relevant areas, thereby leading them to gainful employment, either self or wage, by enhancing their employability.

Today the employers, in general, require trainable, flexible and competent young persons who can adopt and adapt as per the requirements of jobs in the production and service sectors. VET can thus be termed as the basic input essential for social and economic development. Through the supply of willing and competent workforce, the industry, economy and the quality of life can be ensured and strengthened. In most countries, therefore, VET is being seen and visualised as a long-term investment in the national economy.

The system of vocational education and training aims to develop skilled manpower through diversified courses. According to the Government of India (1985), 'Vocational Education has been understood as an education designed to prepare skilled personnel at lower levels of qualifications for one or more groups of occupations, trades or jobs'. The Education Commission (1964–66) was of the view that for a majority of occupations, university degrees were not necessary, and these jobs could be competently performed by trained higher secondary students. The commission felt that it should be possible to divert at least 50 percent of students completing years of education to the VET system, thereby reducing the pressure on the university system, and preparing students for gainful employment. The revised policy formulations in 1992, in addition, envisaged a generic vocational course at the higher secondary stage, which will cut across several occupational fields and is non-occupation specific. The Review Committee (1990) chaired by Acharya Ramamurti of National Policy on Education (NPE) 1986, recommended 'vocationalisation for all'. Encyclopaedia Britannica 1997 defines VET as "instruction needed to equip persons for industrial and commercial occupations. It may be obtained either formally in trade schools, technical secondary schools or through on-the-job training programme or more informally, by picking up the necessary skills on the job".

In India, VET has been proposed as a distinct stream after class X, encompassing major areas of agriculture, business and commerce, engineering and technology, health and para-medical services, home science and humanities and other services.

The National Working Group on Vocational Education (Kulandaiswamy Committee, 1985) reviewed the then prevailing vocational education programme extensively. It defined the concept of vocationalisation at all levels and recommended setting up of a well-knit management system, establishment of linkages among different agencies offering vocational programmes, action plan for promotion of vocational education programmes in the country and liberal grants for attainment of the targets fixed. The NPE 1986 put the target of 10 percent diversion of students to vocational stream by 1990 and 25 per cent by 1995. The revised policy formulations (1992), however, revised the target. For the vocational stream it kept the target of 10 percent diversion by 1995 and 25 percent by the year 2000. The Synergy Group constituted by MHRD, GOI, in 1995 focussed at developing skilled manpower for (a) removing mismatch between demand and supply (b) avoiding duplication and coordinating and integrating efforts of various departments and institutions and non-governmental organisations and (c) keeping pace with the globalisation and consequent induction of new and emerging technologies and developing skilled manpower in related occupations/vocations.

Recently NEP (2020) reimagined vocational education in the context of skills required by twenty-first century workforce. It maintained that "This policy aims to overcome the social status hierarchy associated with vocational education through requiring that ALL educational institutions—schools, colleges and universities—integrate vocational education programmes into mainstream education in a phased manner, beginning with vocational exposure at early ages, quality vocational education through middle and secondary school and progress smoothly into higher education. Integrating vocational education in this way will ensure that every child learns at least one vocation and is exposed to several more, emphasising the dignity and importance of labour and exciting students about various vocations, including those involving local arts and artisanship". Fixing the goal for diversion it said, "By 2025, at least 50% of learners through the school and higher education system shall have exposure to vocational education".

No education today can be accepted as being relevant unless it helps in unfolding the full potential of the child and plays the role of linking the development of the child with the society and its political, productive and sociocultural dimensions. Apart from building up democratic citizenship, developing attributes of critical thinking and creativity and evolving values in a plural society, education today has to develop generic competencies that cut across various domains of knowledge as well as skills and provide training oriented towards skill formation in the context of rapidly changing technology. In other words, this would mean formation of multiple skills, the transferring of learning and ability to continue to unlearn and learn. VET in the Indian context will include:

- Flexible or modular courses of varying durations

- Multiple entry and exit points with in-built credit accumulation facility
- Vertical and horizontal linkages with academic, vocational and technical programmes
- Accessibility from the level of a village cluster to the block and district levels and in urban areas
- Provision of carving out 'work benches' in the neighbourhood out of the existing economic activities, production and technical centres
- Scope of encouraging local farmers, artisans, mechanics, technicians, musicians, artists and other service providers as resource persons or invited faculty
- A decentralised accreditation and equivalence programme, which will also recognise 'work benches' for the purpose of evaluating and certifying students.

VET is multi-sectoral in nature. It is one of the most significant components of human resource development with great potential for adding value to products and services, contributing to the national economy, and improving the quality of life of the people. VET, therefore, needs to be modernised by periodically removing the obsolescence, promoting industry–institute interaction, restructuring of courses and programmes, linking it with developmental sectors and application of science and technology for rural development.

Generally, all over the world, greater prestige is accorded to the study of ideas and abstractions. Much lower prestige is given to practical studies and manual work. Liberal arts have been considered suitable for potential leaders of the society and vocational studies for potential followers. As a matter of fact, it has now been realised at both national and international levels that VET is a 'wise business investment' both for the nation and the individual. India's transition to a knowledge-based economy requires a new generation of educated and skilled manpower with competence in digital technology.

There is a growing demand for skilled workers in various sectors, but this demand is not being met by the existing system.

As a result, there is a mismatch between the skilled manpower required and the skilled manpower available. In order to make the system more responsive to the changing demands, the need is to create a system of VET that is flexible, sustainable, inclusive and creative. It is with this realisation that the Knowledge Commission had to recommend for a flexible VET system in the country. Such a system has to meet the need for skilled manpower for the emerging sectors of the economy in both organised and unorganised sectors. The system has to be geared to prepare students for self-reliance and gainful self-employment. It will have to attract a sizeable student population to varied VET courses aimed at enhancing the individual employability by providing quality skill training in different vocations.

VET has to be approached within the comprehensive concept of human development. In this context, Kulandaiswamy's report on VET states, "Development is a complex process. It is not essentially a matter of heightening the peak; it is one of lifting the base".

Reimagining vocational education, the National Education Policy 2020 visualised "integrating vocational education programmes into mainstream education in a phased manner, beginning with vocational exposure at early ages, quality vocational education through middle and secondary school and then into higher education. Integrating vocational education in this way will ensure that every child learns at least one vocation and is exposed to several more, emphasising the dignity and importance of labour, and exciting students about various vocations including those involving local arts and artisanship".

Delivery Mechanism of VET Programmes

VET in India is delivered through many agencies and government departments, both state and central, as well as voluntary and non-government organisations (NIOS, 2007). While some ministries have their own training programmes to fulfil their internal requirements, there are others who draw trained persons from the general pool of technical/vocational manpower out of other training systems.

School-Based

Within the school system, the integration of work and education begins with primary schooling. The structured and graded programmes of work education start assuming employment preparatory character from the end of upper primary or middle stage. At the secondary stage of education, there is provision for offering pre-vocational courses. The junior technical schools have existed in the educational system of some states.

As a matter of fact, the magnitude of total VET programme in India is difficult to quantify. This is because of its diversity, both in terms of content and delivery, and due to the involvement of the informal sector. In the education sector, VET is offered at the higher secondary level as a separate stream. It covers six major areas of agriculture, business and commerce, engineering and technology, health and paramedical, home science and humanities through over 150 courses throughout the country.

Presently the Government of India, through a centrally sponsored scheme of vocational education, is promoting coordinated action for skill development with the involvement of all key stakeholders at the national and state levels. The Ministry of Education has developed a National Vocational Education Qualifications Framework (NVEQF). This framework is competency based. In this framework, qualifications have been organised according to a series of knowledge, skills and aptitude. The National Skill Qualification Framework (NSQF) levels are graded from one to ten. These levels have been defined in terms of learning outcomes. Learners have to attain the learning outcomes whether they study through formal, non-formal or informal learning. As per UGC guidelines for skill-based education under NSQF, "There will be full time credit-based modular programmes, wherein banking of credits for skill and general education components shall be permitted so as to enable multiple exit and entry. The multiple entry and exit enable the learner to seek employment after any level of Award and join back as and when feasible to upgrade qualifications/ skill competencies either to move higher in the job profile or in the higher educational system. This will also provide the learner an opportunity for vertical mobility to second year of B.Voc degree programme after one year diploma and to third year of B.Voc degree programme after a two-year advanced diploma. The students may further move to master's and Research degree programmes mapped at NSQF Level 8–10".

VET programme at the school stage has the following phases:

- **Work experience/SUPW at primary and upper primary stages.** At the primary stage, it is offered in terms of creative and self-expressional activities, while at the middle stage, it is done in the form of exploratory activities
- **Pre-vocational courses at the secondary stage.** At this stage minimum of two courses are offered to provide vocational readiness
- **Diversified vocational courses at the higher secondary stage.** These job-oriented courses are designed to develop skill competence for both wage and self-employment. Entrepreneurship, environmental education and rural development are integral parts of the course

At Higher Education Level

There are undergraduate-level vocational courses taught in the colleges under a scheme of the University Grants Commission. Recently BVoc. courses have been introduced. Indira Gandhi National Open University (IGNOU) and other state open universities too provide a number of vocational courses.

Other Sectors

Some other major sectors of VET initiatives besides the education sector are the industrial (labour), health, agriculture and business, and commerce sectors. Technician education under the MHRD is imparted in polytechnics in engineering and non-engineering areas. The entire training is institution-based, and sometimes industrial training is also provided. There are about 1,000 polytechnics run by the state governments and private bodies following the curricula prescribed by the state. Community polytechnics mostly located in polytechnics and similar institutions are centres for non formal skill training in rural areas. There are 700 such centres that train about 4.5 lakh young people every year. There is no entry-level qualification, and the mode of training is non formal.

Vocational courses to urban young persons are also provided in Jan Shikshan Sansthan—a central sector scheme providing non-formal vocational courses. There are 108 Jan Shikshan Sansthan located in different parts of the country.

Craftsmen Training Scheme is implemented through about 5,000 government or privately managed industrial training institutes (ITIs) that are approved by NCVT.

Under the Apprenticeship Training Scheme, the facilities available in the organised industry are utilised to provide training under the Apprentices Act (1961). The objective is to utilise fully the facilities available in the industries for practical training.

Enhancing employability of the products has been the key element in all the VET programmes.

The word employability encompasses all of the following:

- A key outcome of education and training
- Skills, knowledge and competencies to enhance the ability to secure and retain a job
- Progress at work and cope with change
- Trainability and adaptability to new demands

Employability of an educated workforce requires broad-based education and training, mastery of basic and portable skills, ability to work in a team, ability to solve problems and use ICT technology, good communication and language skills, learning to pickup skills and proficiency in multiple skills.

The national VET system, therefore, needs to develop the knowledge and skills that will help the workforce become more flexible and responsive to the needs of local labour markets while competing in the global economy. Its goal is to fulfil manpower requirements for sustainable national development and social requirement for employment. The VET programme has to take into account the ongoing emerging social, economic, political and environmental implications of the global trends to keep pace with the needs and the imperative of change in the vocational world.

VET through Open and Distance Learning

VET is also an important component of open schooling. Open and Distance Learning (ODL) offers new opportunities to those learners who have been deprived of such opportunities so far. Its very nature and in-built flexibility offer greater chances of success to a wide variety of clientele in the area of their skill needs. NIOS provides vocational education in about 100 courses. Knowledge, skills and entrepreneurship have been made essential components of the curricula with emphasis on practical skills and on-the-job training in related work establishments.

Distance learning methods can be profitably used to make training and education available at convenient times, at inaccessible places and at reduced costs. However, it is felt that distance learning, as far as possible, should be combined with traditional training methods in order to avoid a sense of isolation of the learner. For wholesome development, it is necessary to ensure opportunities for fullest achievements of all the categories or sections of the people in the country.

In ODL, the teacher and the learner remain apart in time and space, and the use of educational media and technology is prevalent. Unlike a formal system of education, the ODL system is free from constraints of fixed place and timetable of instruction and evaluation as well as fixed entry and exit points. It can, therefore, be self-paced and individualised, thereby providing for learner autonomy. The use of ODL modality gains significance in reaching out to a large number who could not access formal system due to different learning abilities, special socio-economic constraints, rigidities of education system of fixed hours, prior learning, etc. Vocational education and training through ODL are provided at the basic, secondary, senior secondary and post-secondary levels through combining distance education and open learning with vocational training at partner Accredited Vocational Institutes (AVIs).

NPE 1986 emphasised the need to make available non-formal, flexible and need based vocational programmes to neo-literates, school dropouts, persons engaged in work, unemployed and partially employed persons. Special attention has been suggested for women, rural, tribal, handicapped and deprived sections of the society. The World Declaration on Education for all (Dakar Framework, April, 2000) stated that "Every child, youth and adult has the right to benefit from an education that will meet his/her basic learning needs in the best and fullest sense of the term – an education that includes learning to know, learning to do, learning to live together and learning to be. It is an education geared to tapping each person's talent and potential and developing learner's potentialities, so that they can improve their lives and transform their societies". In this context it will be in the fitness of things to quote the conclusion reached at the Second International Congress on Technical and Vocational Education (TVE) held at Seoul, Republic of Korea in 1999.

"Technical and Vocational Education, as an integral component of lifelong learning, has a crucial role to play in this new era as an effective tool to realise the objectives of a culture of peace, environmentally sound sustainable development, social cohesion and international citizenship".

VET—A Global Concern

UNESCO (1974) defined VET as a "Comprehensive term embracing those aspects of the educational process involving, in addition to general education, the study of technologies and related sciences and the acquisition of practical skills, attitudes, understanding and knowledge relating to occupations in the various sectors of economic and social life". In other words, VET cannot be termed as mere technician training. It is essentially education in the broader sense of the term. Practical work and training being important components of VET system, it is intended to prepare people who could work with their brains as well as their hands, who could translate ideas into hardware, who would not merely be superiors of skilled workers but could interact with them to produce new goods and services.

The Second International Congress on Technical Vocational Education and Training organised by UNESCO at Seoul in April 1999 recommended the following to meet these challenges:

I. Improving systems providing education and training throughout life

- Vocational education as an integral part of national education system
- Sound initial education and training to ensure re-trainability
- Flexible access to vocational education throughout life
- Educational and vocational guidance

II. Innovating the educational and training process

- New methods in initial training of teachers and trainers—facilitating the continuous up-gradation of competencies
- Interaction between learning and the world of work through the educational process
- Introducing new information technologies, environmental issues and foreign languages into technical and vocational education
- Entrepreneurship and training for self-employment and employment in small enterprises
- Assessment, accreditation of work experience and certification of standards

III. Vocational education for all

IV. Changing roles of government and other stakeholders in vocational education

- Provision of VET in public and private sectors
- Legislation for VET
- Financing VET including cost sharing and resource generation by institutions

UNESCO and the World Bank have played important roles in reviving and furthering the cause of vocational or diversified secondary education. UNESCO in 1974 adopted an important detailed recommendation concerning technical and vocational education and argued for provision of technical and vocational education as 'an integral part of general education', as 'a means of preparing for an occupational field' and as an instrument to reduce the mismatches between education and employment and between school and society at large.

A joint message from UNESCO and ILO (2002) states "As economic, social and technological change gathers pace, people everywhere need to develop their knowledge and skills, on a continuous basis, so that they can live and work meaningfully in the knowledge society". Clarifying the concept, it states, "Quality technical and vocational education and training help develop the individual's knowledge of science and technology in a broad occupational area requiring technical and professional competencies and specific occupational skills. National TVET systems, therefore, need to develop the knowledge and skills that will help the workforce become more flexible and responsive to the needs of local labour markets, while competing in the global economy". In a time of continuous economic, social and technological change, skills and knowledge become quickly outdated. People who have not been able to benefit from formal education and training must be given opportunities to acquire new skills and knowledge that will give them a second chance in life and at work.

UNESCO-ILO, in their revised recommendations concerning technical and vocational education, stated that technical and vocational education is further understood to be:

- An integral part of general education
- A means of preparing for occupational fields and effective participation in the world of work
- An aspect of lifelong learning and a preparation for responsible citizenship
- An instrument for promoting environmentally sound sustainable development

- A method of facilitating poverty alleviation

It has further been mentioned in the document that VET should:

- Contribute to the achievement of societal goals of greater democratisation and social, cultural and economic development, while at the same time developing the potential of all individuals, both men and women, for active participation in the establishment and implementation of these goals, regardless of religion, race and age
- Lead to an understanding of the scientific and technological aspects of contemporary civilisation in such a way that people comprehend their environment and are capable of acting upon it while taking a critical view of the social, political and environmental implications of scientific and technological change
- Empower people to contribute to environmentally sound sustainable development through their occupations and other areas of their lives

At the international level, it has been recommended that VET should begin with a broad base. This will facilitate horizontal and vertical articulation within the education system and between the school and the world of work. It should be designed such that:

- VET becomes an integral part of everyone's basic general education. It should include initiation to technology, the world of work, human values and work ethics and standards for responsible citizenship
- Students may freely and positively choose vocational courses to pursue their interests and develop skills leading to occupation in various sectors of economy or to further education
- It allows transfers from one field to another within VET system
- Appropriate types of specialisation is readily available to all within and outside the formal system of

education. It may run in conjunction with training in order to permit educational, career and job mobility

- It is available equally to men, women, girls, persons with disabilities and the socially and economically disadvantaged

VET—An Evolving Concept

The first glimpse of an attempt to integrate vocational elements in general education can be found in the concept of Basic Education.

Work Education: A Redefinition of Basic Education

Mahatma Gandhi propounded the concept of Basic Education/*Buniyadi Shiksha*. He intended to harmonise intellectual and manual work for total development—body, mind and spirit or hand, head and heart and to develop desirable work values. The concept made a clear departure from the prevailing bookish nature of education meant for creating cog in the machine or clerks. He wanted to remove the chasm between those working with their hands and those working with their brains. He wanted to develop intelligent workers who could think as well as work. Gandhi termed them as 'thinking fingers'. In his system of Basic Education productive work in the form of a useful handicraft was to occupy the central place with the whole curriculum woven around it. The resolution adopted at the Wardha National Education Conference of 1937 envisaged that "the craft if taught efficiently and thoroughly should enable the school to pay towards the cost of its teaching staff". In other words, the essence of Basic Education was to integrate work with education, immediate environment and life. In 1938 the Zakir Husain Committee gave practical shape to the educational ideas of Mahatma Gandhi in the form of *Nai Talim*. It was then accepted as the national pattern of education for the elementary stage.

In the present system of education, one finds a dichotomy between work and education. Those who produce wealth with their hands do not have opportunities to pursue formal education of their choice, while those who have access to formal liberal education not only denigrate productive manual work but also lack the necessary skills for the same. The Gandhian proposal of Basic Education (*Nai Talim*) was a radical departure from the colonial paradigm. He challenged it by placing productive manual work at the centre of the school curriculum. In the Gandhian view, participation in productive work becomes a medium of knowledge acquisition, developing values and skill formation. Education through work develops the child's head, hand and heart in a holistic manner. It acts as a powerful corrective to the bookish, information-oriented and generally unchallenging character of school education.

Mahatma Gandhi visualised Basic Education as a tool for the development of national consciousness and social reconstruction. The Secondary Education Commission (1952–53) put forward the idea of multipurpose schools with diversification after eight years of schooling. With the implementation of Basic Education many doubts and difficulties were raised. These related to the productive aspect, corelational aspect and the self-sufficiency aspect.

Education Commission (1964–66), following the philosophy of Basic Education, recommended the introduction of work experience as an integral component of general education. Major categories of work activities were to be drawn from (a) basic need areas such as health, hygiene, clothing, shelter, cleanliness, etc., (b) household work, assisting the elders, (c) cleanliness and beautification of surroundings, classroom, school and subject related activities, (d) community work, social service and (e) exploration of the world of work through socially useful and productive activities.

Ishwarbhai Patel Committee (1977) derived the concept of socially useful productive work (SUPW) from the earlier concept of work experience. The committee stressed that such work must not be performed mechanically, but must include planning, analysis, and detailed preparation so that it is educational in essence. It emphasised on having a balance between productive work and social service-related activities. One of the objectives of SUPW was to lead children to increasingly participate in productive work as they go from one stage of education to another, thereby enabling them to 'earn while they learn'.

The National Policy on Education (NPE, 1986) conceived work experience as "purposive and meaningful manual work, organised as an integral part of the learning process and resulting in either goods or services useful to the community". It was intended to be provided through well-structured and graded programmes, comprising activities in accordance with the interests, abilities and needs of students. It was stipulated that the programme be so graded that the level of skills and knowledge get upgraded with the successive stage of education. This experience would be helpful in entering the workforce. The policy provided for pre vocational programmes at the lower secondary stage was directed to facilitate the choice of vocational courses at the higher secondary stage.

The National Curriculum Framework (2005) accepted work as an arena for learning by children, whether at home, school, society or the workplace. Through work one learns to find one's place in society. It is an educational activity with inherent potential for inclusion. The framework, therefore, recommended that the school curriculum from the pre-primary to the senior secondary stages should be reconstructed for realising the pedagogic potential of work as a pedagogic medium in knowledge acquisition, developing values and multiple skill formation.

Prevocational Programme

The Programme of Action (POA) 1986 emphasised that students at the secondary stage should be so prepared that they can choose suitable vocational courses at the higher secondary stage. It stressed the development of vocational interests and attitudes of perseverance and problem-solving in exploring their vocational preferences. POA (1992), in this context, suggested that the existing work experience programme should assume prevocational character at the lower secondary stage such that it gives the student sufficient insight into a particular area of work.

Generic Vocational Course

The generic vocational course (GVC) stated in NPE (1986) aimed at developing those employment-related soft skills that cut across various vocations. These vocation-neutral skills are required by every educated workforce to be successful in their enterprise. The course was to be offered to the academic stream students of class XI and XII.

The centrally sponsored scheme for Vocationalisation of Secondary and Higher Secondary Education (2011) was revised in 2018 and brought under the integrated initiative (*Samagra Shiksha*). The scheme has been renamed as Vocationalisation of School Education (VSE). The revised norms allow a student to complete training in one job role in 9th and 10th standards; followed by another job role in 11th and 12th standards. The scheme is operated within the NSQF, which establishes a system of educational pathways from school to higher education while providing certification of vocational skills.

Integration of Knowledge and Skills

Harmonious development of intellectual and manual skills is essential for the pursuit of excellence. While concepts and generalisations are developed mainly through the knowledge of theory, they get crystallised through practical work. Working with the hand and thinking with the brain go hand in hand in any developmental task. These two processes are not mutually exclusive. When these two functions separately in a society, people get divided into intellectual workers and manual workers. A desirable goal for any progressive society is towards judicious merging of these two in such a way that the pain and drudgery of a worker is transformed to joy of work, economy of time, effort and resources through education and training.

Knowledge has two components, namely recall and recognition. The information that is received is stored into memory. The knowledge is then understood and organised for using later. Application of the understood knowledge, i.e., how, why and when to apply the facts already learnt, comes next. This is termed as the strategic element in the cognitive process. Analysis, evaluation and creating are higher objectives in this context.

Skill, on the other hand, involves a number of chains of movement executed in a particular sequence. It requires the coordination of hand and eye movements. Such a coordinated activity involving different senses, mental abilities and muscular movements develops complete control. Skill achieves its effect with economy of time, effort and resources.

As a matter of fact, skill and knowledge go together. Once we have the knowledge of what, how, when and why to do a particular task, we go to gain proficiency in doing the thing in a most efficient manner. So, knowledge about things is to be applied into being able to do things. Every skill acquisition has a knowledge component associated with it. Strictly speaking, knowledge and skill cannot be sharply distinguished. Skill involves both content and sequence of action. An urge to learn and improve is basic to skill learning. Skill learning can be seen in three distinct phases—cognitive, fixation and autonomous. In the cognitive phase, the learner tries to visualise or intellectualise the skill to be performed. In this phase, the learner can analyse the skill, acquire knowledge about the operations and their sequences and understand the pattern of movement. In the fixation phase, the learner practices the skill in parts. Practising of skill is continued for a considerable period till the incorrect responses are reduced to minimum or zero. Increased speed is an essential factor in the acquisition of productive skills. The third phase, namely the autonomous phase, is characterised by increase in speed of performance. In this phase, doing becomes involuntary and movements autonomous. Through repeated and regular practice, the skill is developed to the autonomous stage of learning. Since a VET programme intends to develop intelligent middle-level workers, knowledge and skills are to be integrated in any vocational programme. Competency becomes the key factor in the evaluation of any vocational product.

Attitudes and Values

Attitudes represent the beliefs and feelings of the people. These affect to a great extent the motivation, self-satisfaction and commitment towards a job. Negative attitude needs to be converted into a positive attitude. However, it is a difficult process since there is always a resistance to change. But every effort is to be made to mould the attitude so that employees feel committed to the organisation, get motivated for better performance and derive satisfaction from the jobs and the working environment. A change of attitude from negative to positive can lead to marked improvement in behaviour and in productivity, thereby leading to better job satisfaction.

Attitudes and values are important components of any vocational education and training programme. Inculcation of positive attitude and desirable values lead to positive behaviour, motivate employees to perform better and help them to learn effectively to improve further. Knowledge, skills and personality qualities developed in a harmonious manner will help in advancing a worker who is capable of becoming a master, willing to work and adjust as per needs, and can go higher up the ladder through further education and training.

Linkage with Industry

VET emphasises development of need-based skilled manpower for different sectors of economy. This need can be met effectively through a strong collaborative linkage between the school and concerned industry. Students undergo specialised skill training on-the-job or on the shop floor in actual work situations. This would help them for wage or self-employment later. The word 'industry' could mean a factory, an agricultural farm, a hospital, a nursing home, a commercial establishment, a production, service-oriented establishment or a professional institution. This linkage may take various forms, for example, professionals from industry may be involved in (a) review and revision of curricula, (b) development of new curricula, (c) development of instructional materials, (d) transaction of vocational curricula and evaluating student's performance. On-the-job training can be given to vocational students in concerned industries or work benches. VET, therefore, needs to be organised by sharing facilities and resources of industries. The linkage can thus be viewed as total involvement or partnership in the implementation of VET.

Levels of Vocational Education and Training

In India, technical and vocational education is provided in the following broad categories of institutions:

a) Institutions of higher professional technical/engineering education
b) Institutions preparing technicians
c) Institutions preparing craftsmen/skilled workers
d) Apprenticeship training programme
e) Schools/junior colleges with vocational stream

State and regional engineering colleges, Indian institutes of technology, university departments of engineering and technology and technological universities provide professional courses in various engineering specialisations. These courses focus on higher level engineering curriculum intended to prepare those who plan, develop, monitor, or evaluate projects and take up consultancy or research assignments. Within the professional category as well there are different levels of engineers. In the system hierarchy, for every graduate engineer there has to be two or three overseers/junior engineers or diplomates. They are the products of diploma-level technical education institutions called polytechnics. Polytechnics provide technician-level courses, and their products take up supervisory positions under the overall guidance of professional engineers. At the lowest level, there are craftsmen training systems meant for training skilled craftsmen in different industrial and technical areas. The products of industrial training institutes are given intensive skill training to work in industries in the organised sector. They are absorbed by industries as skilled workers to handle tools and machines on the shop floor or on the site under the supervision of junior engineers.

In addition to the above three levels of technical personnel being produced by the technical education system, many commissions and committees on education have come to the conclusion that there are no systematic training facilities for the vast unorganised sector of the economy that constitutes about 90 percent of the workforce, the booming service sector within the country and in the global economy of other countries and also for those who would prefer to go for entrepreneurship and self-employment rather than looking for wage employment. The huge dropouts from the formal system enter the world of work without any specific skill training. In order to prepare such middle-level workers and also to raise the quality of services in areas like agriculture, business and commerce, engineering and technology, home science, para-medical, humanities and other services, diversified courses of vocational nature of varying durations have been recommended and later implemented mainly in higher secondary schools/junior colleges all over the country. These vocational courses are run in collaboration with concerned industries. The curriculum for vocational courses is competency-based. These integrate the elements of knowledge, skills, and personal and social qualities. The major focus of vocational courses is on developing vocational readiness and vocational competence for enabling students to utilise the employment opportunities in self- and wage employment sectors by enhancing their individual employability.

Conclusion

Skilled manpower is an essential prerequisite for quality and efficient production, adaptation and use of new technology. Shortages and surpluses are, by and large, found to coexist in the market due to mismatch between skill requirements of the industry and other employing organisations and the skill base of job seekers. This phenomenon of mismatch is likely to become acute in the face of rapid change in the industry and economy. It is, therefore, essential to orient the educational system accordingly. In order to prepare students to sense entrepreneurial opportunities, organise self-employment activity and manage their enterprise effectively, VET trains and educates through entrepreneurship development programme. A major concern of the educational planners, policymakers and implementers are to extend the reach of the vocational programme to all those who need acquisition or upgradation of skills to increase their employability and thereby improve their quality of life. VET should also be taken as dropout intervention strategy to help these children to prepare for life by providing them employable skills. Other groups of people who need to be provided with skill-based education and training include traditional craftsmen and people from marginalised groups like neo-literates, women, those belonging to Scheduled Castes, Scheduled Tribes and the like. The rapidly changing economic and technological environment requires continuous up-gradation of skills of the workforce throughout life. With the increasing emphasis on lifelong learning and vocationalisation for all, alternative strategies are required to be developed for providing opportunities for vocational education and training to different target groups. There is a need for credit-based modular courses of different durations for different target groups, and bringing in flexibility by developing a system which allows for multi-entry and multi-exit. Effective implementation of VET requires a strong institution–industry linkage.

References

NIOS (2007) Vocational education and Training-A Curriculum Framewotk. MHRD, NOIDA.

UNESCO & ILO (2002) Technical and Vocational Education and Training for the twenty-first Century, UNESCO & ILO, Paris.

Wardha (1937) All India National Educational Conference, Wardha Scheme, Wardha.

GOI, MHRD (1986) National Policy on Education, page 18, New Delhi.

UNESCO (1999) Technical and Vocational Education and Training: A Vision For the Twenty-First Century: Recommendations. Second International Congress on Technical and Vocational Education, Seoul, Republic of Korea.

Government of India (1953) Report of the Secondary Education Commission—1952–53. Ministry of Education, New Delhi.

Government of India (1966) Education and National Development. Report of the Education Commission (1964–66). Ministry of Education, New Delhi.

17

Implementation of Vocational Education: Lessons from the Past

Introduction

Vocational Education and Training (VET) is an important element of the nation's education initiative in independent India. The importance and focus given to vocational education in various policy documents are testimony to the fact that liberal and vocational education are inseparable. The two aspects of the education system, namely academic and vocational may well be termed as two sides of the same coin. However, since independence academic stream has flourished well, but in spite of several attempts, vocational education has not been able to attract sizeable number of students. While a robust system of technical education got established due to large-scale industrialisation but in the post-industrial era, the new concept of vocational education comprising large number of wage and self-employment courses particularly catering to the unorganised sector could not take root. The target of diverting 50 percent of the students to the vocational stream till today remains a dream. As a matter of fact, vocational education should be inbuilt into the total education system at all levels such that it becomes a viable alternative to general and professional qualifications. The National Education Policy 2020 too aimed at overcoming "the social status hierarchy associated with vocational education through requiring that all educational institutions—schools, colleges and universities—integrate vocational education programmes into mainstream education in a phased manner, beginning with vocational exposure at early ages, quality vocational education through middle and secondary school and smoothly into higher education". Integrating vocational education in this way will ensure that every child learns at least one vocation and is exposed to several more. During exposure to vocations, emphasis will be laid on dignity and importance of labour. However, linkage among different streams needs to be comprehensively worked out for transferability from one to the other. Compartmentalisation of students into academic and vocational is detrimental to both the students and the system.

Need for Developing Global Workforce

ET, when considered as education in the broader sense of the term, holds the key to human resource development. In the competitive knowledge society of twenty-first century no vocational education can be effective without a strong foundation of general education. Similarly, general education becomes useful and effective when practical and vocational elements are interwoven into it to prepare the learner for the emerging skill-based vocational world. However, the content and process of vocational education have to be continuously modernised in consonance with the changing needs and requirements of the workforce in a global competitive perspective. National Knowledge Commission (2009) also expressed the urgent need to "redefine the critical elements of imparting vocational education and training (VET) to make it flexible, contemporary, relevant, inclusive and creative".

In order to ensure that the country reaps the benefits of its large young manpower, the latter needs to be adequately trained within a VET system that has been systematically planned and rigourously implemented. Such a system alone will harmoniously develop theoretical knowledge along with practical occupational skills. It is important to recollect here that any modern-day developmental task requires working in unison of head, hand and heart. When thinking, doing and feeling go together in a job, the pain of drudgery generally experienced by the workers gives way to joy of work and economy of time, effort and resources.

Conceptually vocational education and training was to be smoothly woven into the general education system with the aim of developing intelligent and flexible middle-level manpower in different sectors of the economy. In this whole exercise, promotion of self-employment and entrepreneurship was to become an important aspect. However, in the absence of vocationally trained manpower, lack of trained and dedicated vocational teachers, no liberal financing and lack of will in administration, implementation of vocational education remained tardy and largely bookish. Obviously, such an implementation devoid of adequate hands-on practical experience and proper on-the-job training could not produce desired manpower having skill efficiency and entrepreneurial skills.

Lacunae in Implementation

Right from the year 1975–76, when in post-independent India the first national document, 'Higher Secondary Education and its Vocationalisation'—A Framework' was prepared in pursuance of the recommendations of the Education Commission (1964–66), a subtle undercurrent of 'clash of interest' was experienced between the erstwhile Ministry of Human Resource Development and the Ministry of Labour as well as among other statutory councils. This hegemonistic tendency proved detrimental to the development of vocational education as an independent discipline in this country. During the same period, however, at the international level, much research was carried out in this area and a widespread popularity of vocational education was noticed in the younger generation in both developed and developing countries. It is significant to quote here the statistics given in NEP 2020, which concluded that only a very small percentage of the Indian workforce, in the age group of 19–24 (less than 5%), received formal vocational education. This figure, when compared with those available for countries like USA (52%), Germany (75%) and South Korea (96%), looks too meager and grossly inadequate.

There is hardly any well-developed system for skill development or skill upgradation in India. It was only in 2013 that NSQF, as a nationally integrated education and competency-based framework, came into existence in India that enables persons to acquire desired competency levels. However, still much needs to be done for giving a boost to self-employment and catering to the needs of the unorganised sector. Too many interests have affected the management of VET. Till date, it has not been possible to develop a separate cadre of vocational manpower specifically trained in implementing vocational courses. Further, the system is starving for manpower who could manage and control the vocational management system either in the centre or in the states.

VET was philosophically conceptualised to be established on a very different pedestal than mere skill training generally being provided in the industrial training institutes (ITI) under the system of technical education within the Ministry of Labour. While ITIs mainly trained students in technical trades for the organised sector, vocational education system was to educate and train the workforce, particularly for unorganised sector. Through a structured and graded programme of work experience up to class VIII, pre-vocational courses in classes IX and X and job oriented vocational courses at senior secondary stage, the system was expected to prepare students who could enter the world of work with sound footing in general education and having theoretical knowledge and practical skills in broad vocational specialisations. The concept was later expanded to include vocational courses at the higher education stage to provide advanced specialisations as well as for ensuring vertical mobility. Entrepreneurship, leading to employment generation was to be given a major focus in vocational studies.

Premature closure of the Bureau of Vocational Education in the MHRD, absence of visionary leadership in the Central Institute of Vocational Education and lack of coordination among different ministries combined with absence of any uniform national or state level vocational authority, proved suicidal for the healthy growth of VET in the country. Seen in this context, the recommendation of the National Knowledge Commission to 'place vocational education entirely under the Ministry of Human Resource Development' is not only a welcome advice but also realistically founded. The 'fragmented management' has done much damage to school-based vocational education so far. It is time that vocational education is taken out of the 'technical education syndrome' and developed as a composite discipline on its own. However, functional collaboration may be worked out at different levels with different ministries and institutions.

Lessons from the Past

In the past, with the introduction of vocational courses all over the country, many appraisals have been made; and many commissions, committees and working groups have reviewed the implementation of VET. Independent research groups have collected data and highlighted the silver linings as well as pitfalls. But, at the national and state levels, instead of introducing desired correctives, the nation safely fell back to the academic curriculum simply because that is the path of least resistance. The academic stream is well-rehearsed and moving ahead satisfactorily with well-established management and implementation system. VET, on the other hand, requires much hard work, imaginative implementation and systematic efforts in order to make it a viable alternative with same prestige and wage structure. The colonial legacy has been so strong that general education-oriented school administrators found it easy to fall back on something they know rather than treading on unknown pastures.

The PSS Central Institute of Vocational Education, as the research and development wing of the Ministry, should collect relevant data periodically and analyse it in order to assess the impact of training on employability. In late eighties, after countrywide deliberations, Management Information System 'MIS on VET' was developed, and the total system was put in place to collect data at the district level and culminating the analysis and synthesis of data at the centre through a mother computer. NIC and NCERT (the author himself was involved) did an enviable job. Empirical evidence about vocational graduates is essential for 'continuous improvement' of the system. Again, in order to assess demand along with training needs and remove mismatch, much money and effort have gone into manpower planning exercises all over the country, percolating up to the district and block levels. 'Handbook for

Vocational Survey Worker' (initiated by the author) guided the conduct of district vocational surveys by each state in almost all the districts of the country. The district-level surveys need to be revived and periodically updated to make them relevant and up to date.

It should always be kept in mind that implementation of VET is costlier, practice-oriented and much diversified than general education. Educational administrators, in general, have not been able to appreciate this added requirement. This has led to a very meager amount of grant being allocated to VET, or even if allocated, the same have largely remained unutilised because of ignorance or over-cautiousness about financial spending. An interesting example came to light in a school where the vocational teacher asked for ten screw drivers. The Principal's Office wrote on the file, 'Buy ten screws from the market; for drivers send the requisition to transport department'. This may be an exaggeration, but the fact is that the general education system lacks professionalism when it comes to vocational education. NPE 2020's recommendation to increase resource allocation to education in general and vocational education is well taken, but its utilisation needs to be monitored by those who are vocationally oriented.

The production cum training centre concept tried by some states in vocational schools, if implemented properly, can help in resource generation. At the same time, such centres within the system can be quite handy to provide much-needed on-the-job practical skills to students. Imaginative and rigorous implementation of the production cum training centre concept can go a long way in augmenting infrastructure, generating resources and training on the job.

In addition, during implementation a few innovative practices came to light about how resources were generated by resourceful teachers and administrators in Madhya Pradesh, Goa, Karnataka, Gujarat and other states. These innovative practices need to be properly identified and thoughtfully documented for others to emulate and further innovate newer strategies. In this context, while making many practical suggestions for resource generation, comments that 'An oft-repeated argument is that if people are ready to pay (higher fee to obtain additional resources) why should it not be accepted. If this argument is taken at its face value, education ceases to be a service'. Let us not forget that Gandhiji's Basic Schools were to be self-sufficient by raising revenue through production and services and not by enhancing fees.

Focus on Unorganised Sector

At this point of history, the need is to go for massive training of prospective workers and working learners in the unorganised sector by exploring new delivery models. The system must ensure quality assurance through national vocational qualifications, certification and accreditation so that the practice component of VET is not compromised in any manner. In the past, it has been stressed and even repeated many times that providing training for entrants in the unorganised/ informal sector in a big way is imperative. However, till today, hardly any long-term solution to the problem has been attempted. The real difficulty lies in the fact that under international pressure, we do initiate some reforms, but do not attempt to solve the real problem. For example, we not only emphasised but also achieved great success in abolishing child labour in India, but no alternative, viable and systematic scheme has been put in place that could compensate the families for the financial loss and simultaneously offer skill-oriented education to prepare them for alternative jobs after attaining the required age. Similar situation prevails in the case of persons working in the unorganised sector. Although we agree that services being provided for our day-to-day life requirements are awful, most of the time unhygienic and based on trial and error, but no organised mechanism at the local or state level has so far evolved to train suitably the unorganised sector worker and also solve financial problems. Efforts to bring them into the mainstream education that is academic in nature either through formal, non formal or distance education does not solve the real problem. In fact, such children when compelled, develop apathy towards education. This 'greatest challenge' requires evolving short-term practical courses along with basic literacy tailored to the job requirements. But this would be possible only with the active cooperation of the employers and the employee's associations. As stated by National Knowledge Commission, "This aspect of VET is critical for the success of the system as a whole". In this context, the latest stipulation of NEP 2020 is particularly welcome when it states, "HEIs will also be allowed to conduct short-term certificate courses in various skills including soft skills".

There is an urgent need to strengthen the current institutional structure. The existing training structures are ill-equipped for the purpose. Administration of vocational education requires unconventional approaches, different genre of trainers, flexibility in terms of time, money, resources and methodologies. Modular courses of flexible durations, open and multi-entry and exit system as well as a judicious mix of practical vocational and academic studies, will be able to accommodate diverse target groups. Community colleges of the USA and ICRDCE, Tamil Nadu, can provide valuable clues for developing such an alternative training system that is responsive to the training needs of the unorganised sector. The working learners would have to be given incentives such as tool kits, facilities for upgradation of skills and knowledge and certification in terms of diploma, associate degree, and so on. These courses will have to be constantly reviewed and re-cast as per the latest national and international needs and standards. A separate certification system for VET is essential to wean it from mainstream technical education and to give it a real vocational base.

Conclusion

The fallacy in our country so far has been two-pronged: one, the domination of the well-established system of technical education on VET and second, our inability to create a cadre of real vocational educators and trainers. Another suggestion worth considering is that the term 'vocational education' may be replaced by another suitable nomenclature like 'skill development' to enhance its acceptability in the society. Unless the 'Fitter, Turner, Carpenter syndrome' is demolished from the minds of the educators and administrators, vocational education cannot take its roots in this country. Vocational is in fact an umbrella term encompassing competencies required by middle-level workers and entrepreneurs in technology, agriculture, home science, para medical, business and commerce and other services. One can only hope that the well-meaning recommendations of the National Education Policy are implemented in letter and spirit to do justice to the distinct field of vocational/skill education. manufacturing and service sector of the country is in urgent need for intelligent middle-level workers having job-based modern training of international standards. No narrow loyalties should be allowed to come in the way of developing a self-sufficient vocational education and training system in the country, which is required to give a competitive edge to our manpower in the global market.

Reference

GOI, MHRD (2020) National Education Policy, 16.3, page 42, New Delhi.

GOI, (2009) National Knowledge Commission, Report to the Nation 2006-2009, New Delhi.

Sen Gupta, M. (1997) Resource Generating Institution. The Hindu, Tuesday, Dec. 2.

GOI, MHRD. (2020) National Education Policy, 0.2, page 3, MHRD, New Delhi

18

Research in Vocational Education and Training: Need, Trends and Areas

With the advent of twenty-first century, followed by post-industrial knowledge-based technological changes, vocational education is poised to undergo complete transformation in favour of twenty-first century skills both in its content and processes. The next generation workers can make the grade in local and global economy only if they are able to think their way through complex and abstract problems, work efficiently in groups and as teams, distinguish and sift useful information and effectively communicate with national and international clientele. In an age when internet is changing the way we learn, think, play and live, to be successful, the workforce across the board will require to be flexible, trainable, adaptable, take initiative, be self-directed, possess sociocultural skills, be productive, remain accountable, provide leadership with responsibility and be well versed in research skills and practices along with the use of multimedia and contemporary technological skills.

Apart from cognitive skills like critical and creative thinking, problem-solving and synthesising information, the members of the workforce also require certain work habits, work ethics and character traits like perseverance, self-discipline, imagination and innovativeness. Environmental conservation, understanding of ecosystems, and alternative sources of energy combined with health, wellness, nutrition and safety are other important concerns in this context. It is argued in knowledgeable circles that "For India, sustainability and ecological aspects should determine the educational model for skills and competence. In the rural context, the vocations are to be sought in the management of environment, water, food, energy, information, human comforts, and reduction of drudgery in work". (Sacheti, 2006). In a similar context, NEP 2020 also mentions that "With the rise of big data, machine learning, and artificial intelligence, many unskilled jobs worldwide may be taken over by machines, while the need for skilled labour, particularly involving mathematics, computer science and data science, in conjunction with multi-disciplinary abilities across the sciences, social sciences and humanities, will be in rapidly increasing demand. With climate change and the rapid depletion of natural resources, there will be a sizable shift in how we meet the world's energy, water, and sanitation needs, again resulting in the need for new skilled labour, particularly in biology, chemistry, physics, and climate science".

In view of this, it seems to be clear that vocational education would require a developmental orientation as opposed to industrial orientation. It is here that research in vocational education and training becomes not only significant but an imperative. In view of the assertion in NEP 2020 that "Vocational education will be integrated into all educational institutions in a phased manner over the next decade" and also the recent introduction of the National Skill Qualification Framework (NSQF), there is need of research inputs for their development and improvement on scientific lines, in terms of duration, curriculum development, curriculum evaluation, curriculum transaction and assessment. Simultaneously there is need to identify the factors responsible for slow progress of vocational education in the country.

Emerging Paradigms in VET

As economic, social and technological changes gather momentum, a need is felt to enhance and add to the knowledge and skills on a continual basis in the areas of production, distribution, innovation and services. Quality vocational education and training positively contribute to an individual's personal and vocational development. It enhances one's productive capacity and facilitates productive participation in economic and social life. Basic general education ensures development of human personality and citizenship qualities and also lays the foundation for future employability by providing general core work skills in a holistic manner. However, vocational education and training further enhance and broaden the scope of employability skills by providing vocation-specific competencies, inculcating entrepreneurial qualities, providing insight into self-employment initiatives and developing industry oriented professional knowledge and skills. In other words, the aim is to facilitate smoother transition of the learner into the world of work. Since in every work field today, ICT has made deep inroads, advanced digital technology as a new dimension has been added to VET. It has proved its potential to improve people's access to VET enormously as well as substantially improving their employability by enhancing efficiency, developing better understanding and increased communication possibilities.

Thus, with the advent of computers, digital technology, mobile technology, artificial intelligence, nanotechnology and revolution in communication technology, the vocational world has undergone rapid and profound changes. Consequently, VET is going through a period of intensive change and reorientation. In independent India, multiple national models, forms, and structures have emerged in an effort to cope with the rapid technological advances and to meet the changing needs of the labour market (Sen Gupta, 2016). With the introduction of NVQF, accreditation and the policy guidelines of NEP 2020, the vocational education and training system are being systematically reformulated and reoriented with an eye toward satisfying the rising demand for a global workforce.

In the present-day context, when the economy is becoming global and competitive, technology is becoming all-pervasive, the profile of the learner is undergoing a perceptible change and a definite rise in the expectations of employers and parents is being felt. The workforce requires high degree of skills in widely diversified vocational fields for maintaining a high pace of economic growth and ensuring quality improvement in the expanding economic sectors. This emerging need obviously calls for a large network of technical and vocational institutions encompassing those of higher professional technical education, institutions preparing technicians, training craftsmen/skilled workers, apprenticeship training programmes and schools/

junior colleges offering vocational streams. Besides, there will also be specific skill development programmes run by specialised industries/business organisations to satisfy their skill requirements.

Issues and Concerns

Shortages and surpluses in manpower demand and supply are found to coexist in the market due to mismatch between the skill requirements of employing organisations and the existing skill base of job seekers. The mismatch becomes acute in the face of rapid structural changes in the economy. Also, another major issue that concerns educational planners, policymakers and implementers today is extending the reach of the vocational training programmes to the unreached that specifically require skills to enhance their employability and thereby improve their quality of life. The vulnerable groups of people who need to be provided with skill-based education and training include traditional craftsmen and people from marginalised groups—neo-literates, women, people belonging to scheduled castes and scheduled tribes, mentally and physically challenged, working learners, migrant workers, etc.

Another important concern is related to the large number of children leaving schools at various stages of education. Retaining these students within the education system right from the post-primary to postsecondary stage has become a major issue. In this context, vocational education and training is considered a 'drop out intervention strategy' to help prepare these children for life by providing them employable skills. Further, the rapidly changing economic and technological environment requires continuous upgradation of the skills of present workers. There is, therefore, a need for training re-training and upgradation of skills of the workforce throughout life.

Thus, in order to reach the goals of 'life-long learning' and 'vocational education and training for all', alternative strategies need to be developed for providing opportunities of VET to different target groups. Credit-based modular courses of different durations must be initiated for bringing in flexibility to allow for multi-entry and multi-exit by students. Effective implementation of VET requires a strong school–industry linkage. The system is also required to train students to sense entrepreneurial opportunities related to their vocations so that apart from wage employment, they are also able to create employment opportunities for themselves and others.

Need for Research

Research is an activity that is directed towards improvement of educational practices. It is a systematic and scientific process of enquiry to discover new and pertinent facts and information in any branch of knowledge. A good piece of research reveals the mismatch between expectation and experience. It tries to arrive at a new and better solution to an existing problem. With the same logic, VET research too aims at finding out new information about various aspects of vocational education and training, including skill formation, skill upgradation, pedagogy of skill learning, institution-based and enterprise-based training, classroom teaching, learning, evaluation, and shop floor practical instruction in different settings and at different levels. A researcher probing into VET enunciates the problem related to the field of vocational education and training, formulates hypothesis, collects the facts or data from both primary and secondary sources, analyses them, interprets, and then reaches certain conclusions either in the form of a solution to the problem or arrives at a generalisation for some theoretical formulation.

Periodical reorientation of our education system in general and the VET system in particular to the changing occupational requirements is an essential condition to keep the system relevant, contextual and effective. This would, however, require an up-to-date database and continuous research inputs on academic as well as administrative aspects of VET. Research-based decision-making and research-based interventions can only lead to a better and satisfactory solution to problems encountered during policymaking and implementation. But evolving such a system requires collection of large pool of valid and reliable data. It also requires valid research evidence, after careful analysis and interpretation of the emerging issues and problems so that the whole process of reorientation becomes scientific, cost-effective and socially acceptable. In fact, such a large-scale reorientation prior to large-scale expansion brings to the fore many unresolved issues and problems related to quality manpower production. These include:

1. What should be the national policy on VET?
2. How to create a distinct cadre of vocational manpower to plan and manage the VET system?
3. How to establish equivalence among diverse vocational qualifications?
4. How to strengthen school–industry linkage?
5. How to ensure vertical mobility of vocational products?
6. Who should teach vocational courses?
7. How to improve acceptability of vocational courses?
8. How to weave in flexibility into the system to make it suitable for varied target groups?
9. What should be the proportion of hard skills, soft skills and generic skills in an effective vocational education and training programme?
10. Is integration of vocational education programmes into the mainstream the only way to overcome the social status hierarchy associated with VET?
11. What should be the mechanism to document and disseminate the innovative practices and successful models in individual institutions?
12. What measures will be required to make the vocational education and training acceptable to the general masses?

These and many other problems related to infrastructural development and implementation require in-depth exploration/investigation through observation, experimentation and other forms of systematic enquiry followed by an objective and penetrating analysis and formulation of conclusions.

Rationale for Research in VET

It is in line with the above perspective that the Programme of Action (POA), – 1992 stipulated that "selected technical and management institutions including IITs, IIMs, RECs and TTTIs (later renamed as NITTTRs) etc. will undertake research and studies on systematic issues concerning educational planning and management, teachers, students, cost-effectiveness, research mobilisation, instructional system-design, curriculum development, examination reforms, etc. and disseminate the findings to all institutions for information and suitable improvements". In India, VET programmes of different natures and durations are provided by the Ministry of Human Resource Development, Ministry of Labour, State Government Departments and several other ministries, NGOs and private providers to develop specific manpower. Vocational courses through ODL have been quite popular both at secondary level, implemented by the National Institute of Open Schooling and at the higher education level by Indira Gandhi National Open University. However, there is a lack of coordination and standardisation.

There is a need to create a central database so that one can have access to data related to various aspects of vocational education and training systems in a comprehensive manner. Also, no systematic policy or any effort in that direction is visible to undertake and promote research in the potential area of VET. Research studies available till date on VET have emanated from NCERT (erstwhile DVE and now PSSCIVE) and from Education faculties of colleges and universities and are mostly in the form of descriptive surveys and status studies or, at best evaluative studies.

Historically speaking, after the discontinuation of multipurpose scheme of secondary education as recommended by the Secondary Education Commission (1952–53), VET got a major impetus in the wide-ranging recommendations of the Education Commission (1964–66), which suggested provision of vocational education right from post primary to post secondary stages. This was followed by NPE 1986 and the accompanying Programmes of Action 1986 and 1992, and now NEP 2020. Vocational courses at the +2 level were started in schools and in junior colleges all over the country in accordance with the blueprint presented in the national document ,'Higher Secondary Education and its Vocationalisation' (NCERT, 1976). Later the efforts became more systematic and objective-based with the introduction of Centrally Sponsored Scheme of Vocationalisation of Secondary Education by the Government of India in 1988. These developments at the national level offered educational researchers a new area of research viz: research in the potential area of vocational education and training.

Research Trends

Initially, during the formative stages series of studies were conducted at both state and national levels, first to select suitable vocational courses and develop their curricula and then to monitor and evaluate the implementation of vocational courses for making mid-term corrections. VET programme in India has been specifically designed not only to meet developmental or manpower needs but also to democratise education and to make it inclusive by broadening opportunities for all to develop their capacities to the optimum level. Discussing the trend of research in vocational education, Sen Gupta (1996) observed an imbalance of coverage of vocational areas in his trend report on 'Research in Vocational Education'. It mentioned that "No study has been reported which is philosophical, analytical, and critical in nature". The trend report on 'Vocational and Technical Education', as documented in the Fifth Survey of Educational Research (1998), concluded that research done during the period hardly paid any attention to issues like sociology of vocational-technical education, comparative studies, the economics of VET, issues of manpower planning, management of VET, curriculum analysis/ evaluation and organisational and administrative issues related to VET implementation. Almost all reported studies during the period lacked any sound theoretical perspective.

In another trend report on 'Work Experience and Vocational Education' Sacheti (2006) maintained that "In work experience, a fair number of programme evaluation studies has been conducted. Issue-based research is grossly inadequate". As regards research in vocational education, the trend report (1993–2000) states that the trend of research was towards status and programme evaluation. Issue-based research was far from adequate. Studies related to vocational choice and follow-up of students were undertaken. Comparative studies were lacking.

Studies in the area of manpower planning, curricular issues and studies on economics of VET were conspicuous by their absence.

A review of research done in India and abroad on topics related to VET indicates that in developed as well as in developing countries, there are several issues and problems which have emerged during the formulation, implementation and reorientation of VET programmes. There are also many conceptual issues related to VET that require research inputs. Over the years, many studies evaluating programme implementation have clearly identified these issues from time to time. At this stage of development, there is a dire need of worthwhile research at the national, regional, state and local levels. Conducting these research, disseminating their findings, effective incorporation of suitable changes and evolving new models should become a continuous feature to transform the VET programme into a dynamic and vibrant system. Such research should be so designed that they address the right and relevant questions. Considering the nature and variety of unresolved issues and problems, particularly in Indian settings, and keeping in view the significance of this spectrum of education for national development, it is found that the volume of issue-based research studies carried out so far in the country is grossly inadequate.

Need to Promote Research in VET

As a matter of fact, research in VET is yet to come of age in India. Its need and importance have not been properly acknowledged by the planners and administrators. There is no systematic attempt to train and promote researchers in this vital area. At the global level, however, one finds serious research efforts in VET in developed countries, particularly in Australia, England, USA and the European countries. Especially dedicated journals on research in VET disseminate their findings regularly. In India, some of the studies done by researchers in the faculty of Education did investigate some issues related to implementation, but VET research as a specialised field is yet to take shape. With the introduction of vocationalisation of education in the country since 1976, research activities were initiated in the erstwhile Department of Vocationalisation of Education in the National Council of Educational Research and Training, New Delhi. These emerged as district vocational surveys, on-the-spot studies of implementation, quick appraisal studies, evaluative studies of centrally sponsored schemes of vocational education and some sporadic individual research. Few post-graduate dissertations and Ph.D. theses also researched topics related to VET under different universities. The Educational Research and Innovation Committee (ERIC) of NCERT too promoted research in the areas of VET. All these efforts were later documented in the Fifth and Sixth Survey of Educational research published by the NCERT in 1998 and 2006. Later the PSS Central Institute of Vocational Education of NCERT continued the task and disseminated these efforts through its *Indian Journal of Vocational Education*. Recently, the School of Vocational Education and Training of Indira Gandhi National Open University has been promoting doctoral research in the area of VET.

Therefore, keeping in view the variety of vocational programmes of varied durations and having different objectives, there are a host of issues and problems that need to be reviewed, researched and resolved. Recognising the vastness of the scope of VET programmes and great variations in their quality, duration and objective it must be said that there is a great dearth of in-depth and rigorously conducted issue-based research for planning and policy formulation as well as systematic outcome-based implementation. Research studies are also required to provide an empirical base for the development of instructional materials, textbooks and resource materials.

Transaction of the vocational curriculum requires extensive research to improve the teaching-learning process. There is hardly any research evidence in Indian settings regarding minimum infrastructural facilities for different courses, provision of right type of teachers and to bridge the gap between industry/business and service organisations and the school/college. A major objective of VET relates to developing entrepreneurship, preparing students for self-employment and training working learners in the unorganised sector. Here again, sufficient research evidence is not available in Indian settings.

Areas for Further Research

It would be desirable to constitute interdisciplinary research teams who should carry out studies regarding manpower requirements, financing of VET, research in philosophical, sociological and psychological foundations of VET, cost-effective strategies, nonformal and distance modes to reach the unreached, pedagogical analysis of skill development, entrepreneurship, self-employment and social rates of return of VET programmes. Valid and reliable research findings emanating from these studies and district-wise collection of data through country-wide management information system (MIS) should be continuously fed back to policymakers, planners, employers, implementers and stakeholders.

Taking a wider view, it is observed that the four major problem areas common to most of the developing countries are (i) acceptance of vocational education option only as a last avenue, (ii) poor utilisation of funds, (iii) lack of coordination (iv) limited industry participation in training and (v) absence of vocationally trained management personnel.

Research in VET will obviously cut across several disciplines. These could be in the form of descriptive/survey type of studies, explorative studies, evaluative studies, analytical or critical studies, experimental studies, case studies, pilot studies, review of research, tracer studies, foundational studies, historical studies, documentary analysis or comparative studies in cross-cultural perspective. In the context of centrally sponsored scheme, one can undertake on the spot studies, quick appraisal studies or follow-up studies. VET has a wide scope and is being implemented in a variety of forms. Hence, there can also be feasibility studies, impact studies, correlational studies, status studies, developmental studies, multicentric studies and even gender-based studies.

In a comprehensive sense, VET research covers research related to vocational awareness, vocational exploration, vocational experimentation and issues and problems related to area-wise specific vocational courses and their implementation. Therefore, the scope of VET research encompasses vocational education and training at different levels of school and college education, vocational education and training done through polytechnics and industrial training institutes, as well as those done by various governmental and nongovernmental agencies for specific manpower development. Vocational courses introduced in community colleges add another dimension in this context.

Thus, while identifying areas of VET, all the above are to be taken into consideration. As stated in NPE 1986, it intends to prepare students for identified occupations spanning several areas of activity to be ordinarily provided after the secondary stage. Emphasis will also be on development of attitudes, knowledge and skills for entrepreneurship and self-employment.

Specific Research Issues and Problems

After discussing the research areas in general, let us now concentrate on specific areas/issues of research in VET. These are as follows:

Status Studies on Vocational Education Initiatives: As discussed earlier, central and state ministries and departments, along with private providers, NGOs and government-sponsored projects, have taken many initiatives over the years to meet specific needs of trained manpower in various sectors. These need to be documented systematically through scientifically conducted studies to get a comprehensive view of the initiatives so that a convergence of objectives, efforts and utilisation of resources can be achieved. By identifying overlaps and assessing their strengths and weaknesses, cost-effectiveness and efficiency can be woven into the system after due monitoring. The findings will also enable exchange of materials and expertise as well as provide data for introducing mid-term correctives.

Programme Evaluation Studies: Every vocational education and training programme requires formative as well as summative evaluation to judge its efficacy, find out shortcomings and suggest ways and means to make the programme effective in terms of its stated objectives. Such evaluations can be done internally or by commissioning external experts/research groups. Data will have to be collected comprehensively through personal interactions, group discussions, study of reports, questionnaires and written statements from parents, teachers and concerned authorities. Rigorously done critical analysis and evaluation go a long way in focusing the programmes and improving different aspects of implementation.

Such programme evaluations can be undertaken at the state, national, institutional or project level. Findings of these evaluations help in proper policy formulation and funding.

Studies on Vocational Preferences/Aspirations/Choices/Interests: Occupational choices, vocational interests, vocational preferences, parental aspirations, vocational opportunities and educational needs of students form yet another interesting area for research. There are many socio-economic factors that influence these. What are those factors? What opportunities are available? What are the potential vocational areas that need to be tapped? How to reduce the mismatch between demand and supply in a particular region? These, and many other questions require research-based probing to establish a VET system on realistic footing.

Follow-up Studies: Follow-up studies and tracer studies of vocational products provide a wealth of information about the courses being offered, teaching methodologies being used, quality of training being provided and relevance of training to the actual work situations. Longitudinal studies of entrepreneurial endeavours, cross-sectional studies of entrepreneurs and success stories can provide vital clues and important directions for entrepreneurship development activities. Studies on job satisfaction, job-related stress, organisational climate, motivational strategies, emotional intelligence, attitudes and career behaviour and the like fall within this category.

Studies on Planning and Management of VET: Evolution of a complete but viable management system to plan, implement, manage and change as per requirements is a crucial input in the promotion of VET. As at present, VET is being managed by personnel deputed from engineering, agriculture or the medical system. A distinct cadre of vocational management personnel has yet to be developed. How to develop a vocational management cadre? What type of training programme will be required for such personnel? Any single-track person, who could be an engineer, doctor, or bank manager, cannot do justice to VET as it includes a variety of vocations of varied nature. Emerging and decaying occupations make the task more challenging. Comparative studies in a cross-cultural context, case studies of successful management systems, approaches of strategic planning and SWOT analysis may lead to many research problems in this area.

Studies on Industry–Institute Interaction/Linkages: "VET, in more than one way, is related to economic development. It cannot bloom in isolation. VET institution and the concerned industry/business/service have to work together for mutual benefit. While this requires certain policy decisions, it is equally important to create databases for taking decisions. It is only through research studies that one can empirically establish skill training requirements, training methodologies, education and training resources, placement initiatives and follow-up" Sen Gupta (2016). The application of new technologies in the world of work is a major challenge for the whole education system. It becomes particularly relevant and important for VET. Courses need to be frequently adjusted to accommodate these changes. Investigations should also suggest ways and means of establishing functional and effective collaboration with industry, business, health and other services. The modalities of collaboration in terms of teacher training facilities, library, the extent of collaboration, identification of sites for on-the-job training and apprenticeship, supervision and evaluation are some other issues to be tackled.

Studies on Entrepreneurs and Entrepreneurship: Many research studies are available in the area of entrepreneurship. These relate to engineering graduates, entrepreneurial qualities, entrepreneurial ventures, young entrepreneurs, or women entrepreneurs. But this area needs to be studied, especially in the context of VET, where there are varied target groups and varied vocational courses. Self-employment is one of the important planks of VET. Entrepreneurial qualities, profile of vocational entrepreneurs, transformational leadership, sustainable entrepreneurship and entrepreneurship in a global context are some of the many sub-areas in which research will be quite useful. There are many blocks to entrepreneurship in our country. How to overcome them? How to develop creativity? Entrepreneurship training is yet another aspect that requires research-based interventions.

Studies on Curriculum: Research is essential for developing a vocational curriculum, its effective transaction and the potential area of curriculum evaluation. Developing a curriculum in a variety of occupations, both existing and emerging, is a challenging job. Research has to be inbuilt into the curriculum development process. How to effectively transact the given curriculum? How modern communication technology can be integrated into the transaction process? Is the curriculum achieving its objectives? In order to answer such questions and to make the curriculum relevant, research inputs are absolutely essential in curriculum-related areas like textbooks, instructional material, PowerPoint presentations, e-learning and e-books.

Research studies are particularly required in pedagogy of skill learning, integration of theory and practice, shop floor training, enterprise-based training, VET through distance learning, teaching-learning models, Effective delivery patterns, etc.

Studies on Vertical Mobility/Future of Students: The National Policy on Education (1986) stipulates that "Graduates of vocational courses will be given opportunities, under predetermined conditions for professional growth, career improvement and lateral entry into courses of general, technical and professional education through appropriate bridge courses". But vertical mobility for vocational products has not been systematically addressed to in the Indian education system. All approaches have been ad hoc so far in the absence of meticulous probing into the question. What type of vertical mobility will help serve the purpose and will be acceptable to the students? Should it be limited to universities, or tertiary institutions will have to be roped in? What curricular and systemic changes are required in this context? Such questions leave the field wide open for worthwhile goal-directed research in the Indian context, where variety is the rule. Research, in this case, will essentially be interdisciplinary.

Experimentation and research are urgently required to reconsider criteria of admission to professional, para-professional, technical courses. There is a need to "design and develop suitable higher diploma or degree courses, design bridge courses to facilitate students' entry into science, engineering, medicine or agricultural streams" (Sen Gupta, 2002).

Studies on Vocational Teachers and their Training: The centrally sponsored scheme of vocational education envisages that "Vocational courses will be conducted with the help of full-time as well as part-time teachers". The absence of quality vocational teachers is a major handicap in the way of implementation of VET. Research studies need to be designed to address issues like 'vocational teacher competencies, present status of VET teachers, profile of full-time and part-time teachers, career advancement of VET teachers, different aspects of pre-service and in-service training of VET teachers, training of teacher educators, Mode of training, etc'.

Studies on Specific Target Groups and Manpower Planning: On the one hand, it is said that VET in the school system has failed since good students do not opt for the courses offered, while on the other hand, there are millions of young people desirous of early entry into the job market. What is wrong with the course offerings? Why do students not prefer vocational courses? Research studies should identify the most vulnerable groups potentially requiring VET, the skill requirements in the area, the type of courses in demand, extent of untrained manpower in the unorganised sector, expectations of entrants about training quality, placement, further education and training requirements, etc.

There should be sector-wise studies about the quality and quantity of manpower required, employment patterns, most sought-after courses, the extent of training facilities available, possibilities of on-the-job training, curricular requirements, etc.

Studies on Introduction and Use of ICT: The introduction of information and communication technology (ICT) is a major concern in VET. Operation of computer-assisted machines, use of educational technology, effective use of e-resources for learning, e-governance, creating databases, teaching mentally and physically challenged children and the like will generate many problems for fruitful research in VET.

Studies on Foundations of VET: Understanding about VET, particularly in India, is inadequate and biased. Philosophical, psychological and sociological foundations are not clearly defined. Economical and social returns of VET are not appreciated by educational administrators in general. Research in these foundational aspects can go a long way in establishing a robust VET system in the country as distinct from general or engineering education. Economics of VET comparative cost-benefit studies and comparative cross-cultural studies of VET are urgently required. Development of valid and reliable tools and techniques for studying different aspects of VET and for different age groups of people in Indian settings is yet another important research area.

Conclusion

A good piece of research should dare to challenge any significant theory, policy or practice. Research in VET can be termed as an aspect of educational research activity that is directed to the improvement of VET foundations, products and practices. In this sense, 'education for all' and 'work for all' can be described as two sides of the same coin. Employability includes developing multiple skills as well as personal and socio-emotional skills and qualities to secure decent work in wage employment or create opportunities for employment through self-employment ventures. Therefore, VET is required for all who need development of skills for increasing their employability. In the backdrop of globalisation, liberalisation and privatisation, the system is looking for a viable, need-based and robust VET programme that can effectively meet the emerging skill requirements in a competitive and cost-effective manner, and also that will be acceptable to degree-conscious clientele.

Very few studies are available on what happens to people once they graduate from a technical and vocational education programme over a period. There is a need to take up follow-up studies and tracer studies at different levels and in different settings. Findings of these studies would provide valuable indications for identifying measures to be taken to bring about better adjustments between education, training and the world of work. There is also a need to develop indigenous tools and techniques for measuring a variety of variables in the area of VET.

VET research concerns with not only the research problems that research scholars undertake for their doctoral or post-doctoral research but it also includes researches undertaken or commissioned by research organisations. They also have to do with researches done by the implementing agencies as a developmental strategy, researches conducted by external and internal research groups to evaluate and monitor the progress, to find innovative ways of accomplishing the goals or doing things better, researches for discovering new relationships and also researches in the foundations of vocational education and training.

References

Sacheti, A.K. (2006) Vocational Education. *Sixth Survey of Educational Reserarch 1993-2000* Volume 1. NCERT, New Delhi.

Sacheti A. K., Verma, A.P. & Mehrotra, V.S. (Eds.) (2005) *Vocational Education and Training: Challenges and Strategies*. March. PSS Central Institute of Vocational Education, Bhopal.

Sen Gupta, M. (1992) *Methodology of Skill Development in Teaching-Learning of Work Experience.* New Delhi: DVE, NCERT.

Sen Gupta, M. (1997) Vocational and Technical Education, *Fifth Survey of Educational Research* 1988–92, Volume 1. August. NCERT, New Delhi.

Sen Gupta, M. (2002) Vocational Teacher Education. *University News*, 40 (31) Aug 5–11, New Delhi.

Sen Gupta, M. (2012) NKC Recommendations on Vocational Education: Need for Implementation. *University News*, 50 (34) August 20–26, New Delhi.

Sen Gupta, M. (2014) Revamping Educational Research in Universities. *University News*, 52 (39) Sep–Oct New Delhi.

Sen Gupta, M. (2016) Research in Vocational Education and Training. Indian Journal of Vocational Education, April 2014–May 2016, Vol. 20 & 21, PSS Central Institute of Vocational Education, Bhopal.

Sen Gupta, M. (2017) *Skills for Employability-a Handbook*. New Delhi: Innovative Publication.

Simpson, E.J. (1966) *The Classification of Educational Objectives, Psychomotor Domain*. Urbana, IL: University of Illinois, p. 110.

Singh, Pritam (1983) *A Monograph on Improving Practical Examinations in Science*. New Delhi: NCERT.

19

Teaching Strategies for Vocational Education

Teaching

Teaching refers to the actions of a teacher and learning is the outcome of teaching. All teaching need not result in learning and all learning cannot be attributed to teaching. In other words, teaching is an activity on the part of one person intended to facilitate learning on the part of another. It is not simply cognitive but also covers values, disposition, attitudes and character.

Vocational education and training encompass various kinds of education and skill development activities undertaken at different levels of education. The whole spectrum ranges from post primary to tertiary through both formal, non formal and distance learning programmes in government as well as by private institutions and organisations. In such a diverse scenario, one can easily discern:

- Mismatch between skills provided and skills required by the industry
- Revision of course curricula lagging the requirement of the industry
- Out-dated machinery/tools and technology
- Skill demands of services/unorganised sector remain largely unmet
- Unsatisfactory employability of trainees because of poor quality of training

- Shortage of trained instructors and low instructor training capacity in the country
- Low prestige attached to vocational training.

Of all the hard jobs around, one of the hardest is being a good teacher. Society always looks for a teacher who is competent and committed, whose integrity is beyond doubt and under whose care and guidance the child develops into a good human being, a good citizen, a good worker, and an efficient change agent. With the quantitative expansion in schooling facilities, number of teachers has increased. Education being a fundamental right today, every child is expected to come into the education fold.

Unfortunately, emphasis on massive quantitative expansion and that too in a hurry led to induction of unscrupulous investors, opportunistic middlemen, incompetent teachers and money-minded selfish educators. This invariably attracted reaction from the society and the system. As a consequence, we observe the cutting down of full-time teachers, introducing para-teachers, contract teachers, *shiksha mitras, shiksha sahayaks or guruji's*. This obviously led to the mushrooming of coaching classes, especially in general education sector. With the COVID-19 pandemic, online classes and courses emerged in a big way. Students, too, are found to be running after opportunities rather than being seekers of knowledge.

Vocational Teacher

Dynamic and efficient performance of vocational teachers is crucial in the context of skill education. As we know in the ultimate analysis, it is the right selection, effective training, teaching competence, intrinsic motivation along with conducive conditions of work that impinge directly on teacher's performance. A vocational teacher should be conversant with modern teaching techniques that stimulate exploration, experimentation and work practice on the part of the skill learners. Being a facilitator, the teacher should lead the students to discover efficient and effective ways of performing and thus learn by their own actions. In other words, to keep pace with the societal expectations by inculcating in students the desired quality of performance, the vocational teacher must be more than a communicator or an information dispenser. They have to be a motivator, an effective facilitator, a guide, and a role model.

The vocational trainer is supposed to be a content/trade specialist, an efficient practitioner, capable of developing curriculum and instructional material in new areas and an evaluator of students' performance. They should work as a guidance counsellor to the students, keep a liaison between the school and the community/industry and facilitate learning on the job and placements. They will be required to manage the resources, coordinate with other departments, institutions, and industry, and keep necessary records. Therefore, the vocational teacher will require not only content-specific competencies but also competencies related to foundations and principles of vocational education, effective communication, comprehensive evaluation, guidance and counselling and suitable instructional strategies for both classroom and shop floor.

Vocational teachers have to use hardware in the form of equipment and machine and work on variety of software. Hence, they must acquire necessary expertise to use both effectively and efficiently. While giving instructions in the classroom, assisting and directing students' practical experiences on shop floor and their experimenting in laboratories, farms and factories, the vocational teacher should follow the special methods and techniques of teaching vocational subjects and improvise interactions to encourage student-centric learning. In other words, they have to act as a potent agent of change and a facilitator.

Teaching in this information age will have to create a dynamic learning environment in the classroom and shop floor wherein students are stimulated, challenged and motivated to self-directed learning. Sustained efforts will be required on the part of the teacher to shift from directed learning to student-initiated learning. The vocational teacher has to liberate themselves from the authoritarian role in the classroom. They will empower the learners to assume the pivotal role and enable them to be active partners in the learning process. In addition to having mastery in content, the vocational teacher/skill trainer must also appreciate the scientific nature of the learning process and factors that make learning functional and meaningful. All-round development of human beings is the main objective of the educational process. The development and changes in children occur gradually over a period. The outcome may be observed in the form of acquisition of knowledge, development of understanding, inculcation of desired human values, creation of interest and attitude and the ability to perform the desired skills. Ultimately, these developmental outcomes enable individuals to think logically and rationally for leading a purposeful and socially productive life.

Another important aspect of vocational education is its emphasis on entrepreneurship and self-employment. Hence, in addition to knowledge and skills, students of vocational education would require desired personal qualities like self-confidence, problem-solving abilities, innovation and risk-taking behaviour. Vocational teaching requires more of pupil's involvement in doing things.

In an open and distance learning set-up, vocational courses will be housed in accredited vocational institutes. These institutes will be developed as a resource centre with all resources required for ODL. Skills can be conceptualised in computer-simulated lessons and practised in simulated conditions. There will also be a compulsory component of on-the-job training in actual work situations in specialised industries and enterprises. It will, therefore, be a collaborative model. Those working learners who are good at practice will be given required theoretical instruction, and those who are theoretically oriented will get intensive practice in workbenches. Instructional process related to VET in ODL, thus, will be a combination of specialised lectures and demonstrations through video. Students will receive theoretical lessons through video conferencing and acquire basic skills in the accredited centres. Intensive practice will, however, be provided in related industries and enterprises.

Following competencies are to be developed in vocational teachers with specific reference to instructional process in VET:

- Ability to develop annual, unit and lesson plans

- Select and apply methods like demonstration method, discussion method, project method, problem-solving method, team teaching and lecture method
- Use different teaching techniques like questioning and illustration
- Organise demonstrations and lectures by experts
- Prepare, select and use appropriate instructional material
- Plan and conduct online classes
- Prepare and offer online courses
- Conduct group discussions
- Use feedback techniques
- Operate with dexterity the computer and audio-visual aids and use various types of software
- Develop and use multimedia packages
- Use distance learning mode effectively for teaching and training
- Organise both theoretical and practical examinations
- Record student's progress and performance
- Develop and prepare appropriate tools like rating scales, questionnaires, theory papers, worksheets, checklists and observation schedules
- Use modern media techniques.

It is evident from the foregoing discussion that vocational courses and their effective conduct place special demands on the vocational teachers. They require, in addition to an insight into the philosophical and sociological foundations of vocational education, a thorough knowledge of respective content areas, as well as intensive skill orientation for successful conduct of practice sessions. Pedagogy of learning skills is an important area to be understood and practised by any vocational teacher.

Effective Skill Learning

"Learning of skills involves a series of behaviours arranged carefully in time. A proper sequence of stimulus-response chains is essential to successfully perform the skills. Some skills are best learnt by 'whole' method, whereas there are others in which 'part' method is more appropriate. However, one thing is very clear that 'to be proficient in a skill, repeated practice is necessary'. Through repeated and regular practice, the skill is learnt up to the autonomous stage of learning. Feedback, an essential component for skill learning, enables the learner to compare his performance with some standard or model" (Sen Gupta, 2017).

The three basic conditions for ensuring effective skill learning are coordinated action and proper sequence or contiguity, repeated practice and feedback or knowledge of results. The process will include proper timing, right coordination and proper order. In order to efficiently perform a skill, it is essential to maintain proper sequence of the stimulus–response units and the chains of movements. These movements are to be executed in close-time succession based on a particular pattern. Another basic condition of skill learning is continuous feedback. It enables the learner to compare his performance with some standard of performance.

In the process of skill learning, one can discern three distinct phases, namely the cognitive phase, fixation phase and autonomous phase. In the cognitive phase, the learner tries to visualise or intellectualise the skill to be performed. As he moves to the fixation phase, following systematic instruction and demonstration, the learner starts practising the skill in parts. This is followed by repeated practice over a considerable period, leading to minimum or zero incorrect responses. In the acquisition of productive skills, increased speed of performance becomes an important factor. This happens in the autonomous phase, where increase in speed leads to further control and precision in performance. Finally, doing on the part of the learner becomes involuntary, and movements become autonomous.

A skilled person makes no unsuccessful or unnecessary movements. Hence, economy of movements is a real index of successful skill development. The more skilful the movement, the less work is done and easier the action appears. The skill now becomes more precise, the learner's actions become automatic, and they reach the stage of mastery.

Instructional Strategies

Skill teaching, to be effective, requires sequential presentation in a practical and lucid manner. Demonstration plays a significant role in skill development. A skill should be demonstrated slowly, pointing out the likely mistakes and pitfalls. During demonstration, safety precautions to be observed are stressed. Learners' participation should also be ensured in this process so that immediate feedback can be provided. As a general principle, during skill learning, 'new movements/ skills should be introduced through demonstration followed by students practising the skill under supervision. Every effort should be made to integrate knowledge and skill or thinking and doing for ensuring progressive improvement in accomplishment. In the ultimate analysis, however, students should be left free to articulate and, if possible, innovate using their acquired powers to carry out plans on their own initiative.

Extraneous motivation, like rewards and punishments in terms of good or bad marks, prizes or penalties, also plays a part in this process. Although competition provides a good motivation, but at the same time it has also been experienced that a non-competitive, cooperative and mutually helping classroom climate is more conducive to skill acquisition. It is, therefore, argued that competition between groups and cooperation within the group may prove to be a better dictum to follow for optimum results.

Evaluation of Skill Learning

Evaluation of skill development involves an appraisal of both process and product. The main characteristics of expert performance can be summed up as a steady and uniform flow of motion, easy and economical movements, relaxed performance, concentration on the task and intelligent use of the senses. In a productive activity, a finished product may be judged as excellent or best if it has been accomplished in minimum time, with minimum effort, least wastage of resources and fulfils the saleability criteria. Due weightage should be given to inputs of imagination, originality and persistence on the part of the performer. In a comprehensive evaluation scheme, the emphasis should be on testing of skill attainment by the learner and not on mere acquisition of the knowledge of skills. A variety of evaluation devices will have to be judiciously used to test knowledge, skill, application and the personality traits of the learners. At the end of skill learning, summative test designed for assessing the attainment of all the objectives may be given. Use of different types of tools and techniques for evaluation ensures comprehensive evaluation.

Reference

Sen Gupta, M. Skills for Employability A Handbook, Innovative Publication, New Delhi.

20

Integrating Vocational Education into the Mainstream: A Policy Imperative

Introduction

Vocational education and training (VET) has been termed as important for economic growth and national development. The two streams of academic or liberal education and vocational education should prosper side by side not only to make the system of education inclusive but also to prepare the next generation for both life and livelihood. However, both require systematic implementation throughout the education system. As a matter of fact, vocational education should be inbuilt into the total education system at all levels such that vocational qualification becomes a viable alternative to general and professional qualifications. The National Education Policy (NEP) 2020, in this context, stipulated to "integrate vocational education programmes into mainstream education in a phased manner, beginning with vocational exposure at early ages, quality vocational education through middle and secondary school and smoothly into higher education". Integrating vocational education in this way will ensure that every child learns at least one vocation and is exposed to several more. The inputs will be so designed that work and vocational education at every stage duly emphasise on the dignity and importance of labour. However, linkage among different streams needs to be comprehensively worked out for transferability from one to the other. Compartmentalisation into academic and vocational streams is detrimental to both students and the system of education and training. Such rigid streaming focusing largely on dropouts, combined with a lack of vertical mobility for students from the vocational education stream ultimately led to the creation of a social status hierarchy in which vocational education stream has been perceived by the society as inferior to mainstream education. In their view only those students opt for vocational stream who cannot cope with the mainstream education.

Although this is the first time that the idea of integrating has been stipulated in a policy document, similar recommendations could be found in the reports of a number of commissions and committees set up earlier to review the total programme. As an example, the Ramamurthy Committee (1990) that reviewed the National Policy on Education 1986, recommended linking work with the school through a common curricular stream. This stream will have both vocational and non-vocational components. The curriculum will give different options with varying proportions of the two components. (Sen Gupta, 2021). According to the committee report, "Vocationalisation of school education must be seen in the context of equity and social justice, contrary to the present system where the vocational stream is clearly viewed as the one meant for the less able and the less fortunate". Even earlier, the National Review Committee on Higher Secondary Education with Special Reference to Vocationalisation (Adiseshiah, 1978), in its report titled *Learning to Do: Towards a Learning and Working Society,* recommended flexibility between general and vocational education streams. It suggested different models in the offering of electives.

A close look at the recommendations mentioned, points to the fact that education and skill training is not exclusive, but they fall within the holistic concept of human resource development. Strictly speaking, general education aiming at intellectual, ethical, emotional and socio-cultural development and skill education through VET aiming at industrial and economic development are complementary to each other.

Harmonious Blending of Theoretical and Practical

VET, when considered as education in the broader sense of the term, holds the key to human resource development. In the competitive knowledge society of twenty-first century, no vocational education can be effective without a strong foundation of general education. Similarly, general education becomes useful and effective when practical and vocational elements are interwoven into it to prepare the learner for the emerging skill-based vocational world. However, the content and process of vocational education have to be continuously modernised in consonance with the changing needs and requirements of the workforce in a global competitive perspective. National Knowledge Commission (2009) also expressed the urgent need to "redefine the critical elements of imparting vocational education and training (VET) to make it flexible, contemporary, relevant, inclusive and creative".

In order to ensure that the country reaps the benefits of its large young manpower, the latter needs to be adequately trained within a VET system that has been systematically planned and rigorously implemented. Such a system alone will harmoniously develop theoretical knowledge along with practical occupational skills. It is important to recollect here that any modern-day developmental task requires working with hands and thinking with brain to go together. Any attempt to separate these two will tend to divide the people into white-collar and blue-collar workers. In any progressive society, it is desirable to merge these two judiciously such that the pain of drudgery gives way to joy of work and economy of time, effort and resources. Conceptually, right from the beginning, vocational education and training were to be smoothly woven into the general education system with the aim of developing intelligent and flexible middle-level manpower in different sectors of the economy. In this whole exercise, promotion of self-employment and entrepreneurship were to become an important aspect.

Evolution of a Viable System

Right from the year 1975–76, when in post-independent India, the first national document, 'Higher Secondary Education and its Vocationalisation'–A Framework, was prepared in pursuance of the recommendations of the Education Commission (1964–66), efforts have been made in our country to create a system of vocational education and training along with a separate cadre of management and teachers. Unfortunately, the efforts have been sporadic, ad-hoc and cautious. While there have been pockets of success in few states, it could not lead to the development of vocational education as an independent discipline in the country. During the same period, however, at the international level, much research has gone into this area, and a widespread popularity of vocational education is noticed in the younger generation in both developed and developing countries. It is significant to quote here the statistics given in National Education Policy 2020, which concluded that less than 5 percent of the Indian workforce in the age group of 19–24 received formal vocational education. This figure is too meagre and grossly inadequate when compared with developed countries like USA or Germany.

There is hardly any well-developed system for vocational skill development and skill upgradation in India. Much needs to be done for giving a boost to self-employment and catering to the needs of the unorganised sector. Too many interests have affected the management of VET. Till date, it has not been possible to develop a separate cadre of vocational manpower specifically trained in implementing vocational courses that could manage and control the vocational management system either at the centre or in the states. VET was philosophically conceptualised to prepare intelligent middle-level workers having both theoretical and practical training rather than mere skill training as was being done in technical trades within the industrial training institutes under the system of technical education. While ITIs mainly trained students for the organised sector, vocational education system was to educate and train the workforce in unorganised sector.

Through a structured and graded programme of work experience up to class VIII, pre-vocational courses in classes IX and X and job oriented vocational courses at senior secondary stage, the system was expected to prepare students who could enter the world of work with sound footing in general education and having theoretical knowledge and practical skills in broad vocational specialisations. The concept was later expanded to include vocational courses at the higher education stage in colleges and universities to provide advanced specialisations as well as for ensuring vertical mobility. Entrepreneurship leading to employment generation was to be given a major focus in vocational studies.

Evolution of a viable system of vocational education at par with general education system has not been possible so far. The recommendation of National Education Policy 2020 for constituting a National Committee for the Integration of Vocational Education (NCIVE) has to be seen in the backdrop of implementation under CSS in different states and union territories. Simultaneously cognizance has to be taken of innovative practices adopted and school–industry linkages developed till date, models of implementation adopted in states, apprenticeship scheme already offered, and infrastructure already created in government and private institutions. The Secretariat of the proposed NCIVE (a highly representative body with a wide base) should be housed in the Central Institute of Vocational Education under NCERT, which was created in Bhopal basically for this purpose. What is required is a thorough review of its functioning and restructuring it into an institute of national importance covering total vocational education cohort within the organised as well as unorganised sectors.

A Step Forward

The basic objective with which the Policy has suggested the reform namely removing the stigma attached to vocational stream and achieving the laudable goal of diverting at least 50 percent of learners through the school and higher education system and giving them exposure to vocational education—with the policy statement "Vocational education will be integrated into all educational institutions in a phased manner over the next decade" can definitely be termed as a step forward. Also, addressing the issue of vertical mobility of vocational students through NSQF is definitely another laudable goal-directed step. Yet another praiseworthy stipulation made for the first time by NEP 2020 is that higher education institutions are required to conduct short-term certificate courses in various skills, including soft skills. While the policy has struck the right chord by its focused recommendations, only time will tell whether the step taken is in the right direction.

Conclusion

It is time that vocational education is taken out of the 'technical education syndrome'. It should develop independently as a composite discipline encompassing health and para-medical, yoga and physical education; business, management and commerce; home science and institutional/ event management; agriculture and allied services; education, entrepreneurship and other services and computer and digital technology. However, functional collaboration may be worked out at different levels with different ministries and institutions. Further innovative models and practices evolved by the system in different states and union territories need to be systematically documented, studied and lessons drawn for further refinement of the programme.

References

Adiseshiah, Malcolm S. (1978) *Learning To Do: Towards A Learning And Working Society.* Report of the National Review Committee on Higher Secondary Education with Special Reference to Vocationalisation Ministry of Education & Social Welfare, Government of India, New Delhi.

National Education Policy, (2020) MHRD, Government of India. New Delhi.

Ramamurti. Committee (1990) *Report of the Committee For Review of National Policy on Education 1986,* New Delhi.

Sen Gupta, M. (2021) Integrating Vocational Education into Mainstream: A Policy Perspective. *Indian Journal of Vocational Education,* Vol. 29-31, page 139-145.

Section 4

Teaching and Learning

21

Teaching, Education and Knowledge: Conceptual Analysis

Teaching, education and knowledge are inter-related. However, conceptually they have their distinct characteristics. Teaching includes the inculcation of values, attitudes, dispositions and character building apart from imparting content knowledge. It involves communication and interaction with learners, using a set of teaching skills. Teaching has to be contextual and should enable learners to be active participants in the process of knowledge creation. Teaching being an educational activity, it passes on to the learners something worthwhile and of value in a morally unobjectionable manner. It involves knowledge, understanding and cognitive perspectives in a coherent manner and implies commitment, care and concern.

Education today has become a fundamental right. Providing quality education to the next generation has become vital for survival. But this requires a clear understanding of the nature of knowledge, the meaning of education and the significance of teaching, especially when the whole educational system is undergoing transformation in the face of knowledge explosion, revolution in communication technology and diversification. Human beings, over time, have developed many bodies of knowledge, which include repertoire of ways of thinking, ways of feeling and ways of doing things thus constructing more knowledge. In today's classrooms, knowledge is not considered as a finished product. Instead, more importance is being given to the process of knowledge creation. To a modern teacher, it is important to internalise conceptually terms like teaching, training, instruction, conditioning, education and knowledge, so that they can fruitfully contribute to the development of a productive democratic citizen.

In view of the above, the author has tried in this chapter to analyse the three concepts from different angles to identify their distinct identities as well as to establish their relationship in the curricular context.

Teaching

Teaching is a comprehensive term having a broad cognitive perspective. It involves communication with the learners, beautifully termed as a 'soul-to-soul exchange of ideas'. In the learner-driven education system of today, teaching as a profession has grown into a complex process. It has moved from transfer of information and passive reception to construction of knowledge and active participation. Preaching is not synonymous with teaching because a teacher is expected to practice what they teach. In that sense, they are experienced practitioners. India had great teachers in the past. Teaching was their life's mission. They were living examples of austere lifestyles, internal integrity and character. Later, however, as the number of teachers, students and schools increased and educational system got democratised, teaching came to be considered as a profession very much like medical or legal. It inherently meant professional training with a view to developing competence, commitment, conviction and positive attitude in the teachers. Even though there are many who still consider teaching a vocation, i.e., a means of livelihood or a source of income. There are yet others for whom it is an occupation—a means of occupying their spare time for 'social service' (Sen Gupta, 2021).

Classroom Teacher

A classroom teacher, in the process of teaching, raises questions, encourages questioning and emphasises gathering of experience through exploration, experimentation and work practice in the pursuit of knowledge. They cultivates in pupils the quality of aspiration. They have a deep understanding of the nature of the pupil. They guide the development of the budding organism by giving them the love of a mother. At the same time, in this intricate process of development, they maintain the patience of a father.

A teacher has to keep in mind that students learn in variety of ways. They learn by experiencing, making things, experimenting, reading, discussing, asking questions, listening, thinking, reflecting expressing in speech and by writing. Hence, teachers have to use a variety of strategies in a classroom. These may include lecture, lecture cum discussion, lecture with demonstration, teaching in teams, discussion in groups, mutual exchange of information, ideas and experiences, projects and assignments and presentations. Conferences, seminars, focus group discussions, panel discussions, field trips, team teaching, online classes, webinars, brainstorming sessions and internet surfing can be gainfully utilised to make the process of communication effective.

Complete teachers are those who are masters of their subject, keep their own knowledge updated, have equal command over theory and practice both. They set an example of integrity, character and morality, practise impartiality and learn along with students. They effectively communicate, use modern technology and develop in students the required soft skills. They maintain a safe and secure classroom climate and skillfully manage all events and activities. They are required to develop curriculum and textbook, provide the students required guidance and comprehensively evaluate their performance.

Finally, a teacher is accountable to the society. As somebody has aptly described it: "Lawyers live on the lies of the people, Doctors live on the diseases of the people, Engineers live on the prosperity of the people, but a teacher lives on the *Trust* of the people. Therefore, he must respect the trust bestowed upon him by the people through his conduct both within and outside the classroom".

Education

Education is interpreted differently by different people. Economists consider education as a commodity. According to them, it is profitable for the community to invest in it. Sociologists view education as a powerful tool for socialising the next generation. From a psychologist's point of view, education goes to develop a wholesome personality and sound mental health. Educationists, on the other hand, believe that education, intrinsically conceived, relates to processes in which a desirable state of mind develops.

Human growth is a natural process. Education aids and accelerates the process of growth and development by using deliberate processes and methods. The subject areas help to build bridges between the past and the future through accumulation of experience and transmission of lessons. However, effective education requires a harmonious blending of natural processes and deliberate processes. Education enables unfolding through the process of concentration, inward gaze of consciousness and through progressive discovery of inner self.

There are different models of education in vogue. For example, the 'utilitarian' model of education emphasises those aspects of education that are useful for life and livelihood. The 'moulding' model of education considers education in terms of producing something external to the activity itself. Teacher, according to this model, moulds the personalities of the children. However, a 'growth-oriented' model likens education to a natural process in which the individual develops like a plant. According to this model, education facilitates development of potentialities from within rather than moulding them from without. Education and its system get influenced by political, social and economic philosophy of a country. It reflects the current and future needs and aspirations of the society as well as its lasting values and cultural heritage. Learning to learn and the willingness to unlearn and relearn are important as means of responding to new situations in a flexible and creative manner. Education must develop the ability to work and participate in economic processes and social change. It provides the means and opportunities to enhance the individual's creative expression and the capacity for aesthetic appreciation.

Education and Training

A person may be highly trained but not educated. They like a cook, maybe passionately committed to the skills and exercise them with intelligence and determination. But if they have a limited conception of what they are doing and do not see the connection of their specialised competence in a broader cognitive perspective, they cannot be called educated. In other words, to be termed 'educated', one must be able to see one's specialised competence on a broader canvas, i.e., in a cognitive perspective. There are thinkers who do not agree that education consists in transmission of a body of knowledge. According to them, worthwhile things cannot be forced on reluctant minds. They stress more on critical thinking, individual experimentation, and problem-solving abilities. These are acquired by contact with those who have already acquired them. To that extent, education involves initiation of people to what is valuable in an intelligible and voluntary manner by creating in them a desire to achieve it. Teachers and students together participate in the shared experience of exploring a common world. The teacher is simply more familiar with its contours and more skilled in handling the tools and appraising the nuances. To be 'educated' is not to have arrived at a destination. It is a continuous travel of gaining experiences and internalising them in a creative manner.

'Education' may have within itself elements from training, instruction and conditioning amalgamated in different proportions, but each of these is a distinct concept. For example, education and training although related, are distinguishable. As said earlier, education includes processes that have a wider cognitive perspective.

In training, the cognitive perspective becomes narrowly conceived, for example, we do not educate a person to run a machine, ride a horse or drive a car. When we talk of training, the field of activities becomes more specialised. Worthwhileness of the task is another important criterion. One can be trained in burglary, pickpocketing or even torturing, but since the activities do not come within the ambit of worthwhileness in a societal context, the term 'education' cannot be used to refer to them.

Therefore, any activity to be called 'education' must satisfy three criteria, namely worthwhileness, cognitive perspective and caring. In other words, education implies that something valuable (worthwhile) is being imparted. An individual who is educated 'cares' about the valuable things. They possess relevant knowledge, skills and competence. An educated person is one who has acquired worthwhile knowledge, understanding and skills. Education regards some knowledge and some skills as worth passing on to the next generation. This body of knowledge and skills, in fact, constitutes the syllabus.

Knowledge

What is 'known beyond doubt' is knowledge. This is called conceptual knowledge. It is different from knowledge perceived or experienced through senses. Knowledge deduced from sense experience is always probable knowledge, not certain knowledge. Sense perceptions are often distorted, and observations are always subjective. Even otherwise, the fact remains that things always change.

According to rationalists, true knowledge is knowledge of forms or ideas. Such knowledge does not depend upon experience. It is derived from self-evident axioms or principles. Propositions of this type are 'a priori' and necessarily true. Mathematics and logic are the paradigms of this type of knowledge. Empiricists view knowledge as 'a posteriori'. Here, knowledge is not taken as a matter of deduction, but as a result of observation and experimentation in the empirical world–the world of sense experience. This substantial truth is not a body of necessary truths, but of conclusions or generalisations based on observation and experience. These may not happen in the same manner always under all conditions. There is no 'necessity' about these truths. They are truths that are contingent. Negation of any empirical truth is always possible. But negation of mathematical truths is logically impossible and absurd. According to empiricists, knowledge is obtained through sense experience. This knowledge is about the world of objects or phenomena. It is a posteriori based on human experience. Science is the paradigm of such knowledge.

As per the National Curriculum Framework 2005, knowledge is conceived as experience organised through language into patterns of thought or structures of concepts, thus creating meaning which in turn helps us to understand the world we live in. It can also be conceived of patterns of activity or physical dexterity with thought contributing to acting in the world and creating and making things. Human beings, over time, have evolved many bodies of knowledge, which include a repertoire of ways of thinking, feeling, doing things, thus constructing more knowledge. All children have to recreate a significant part of this wealth for themselves. They therefore learn to participate in the very process of knowledge creation. In this sense, knowledge is not only the product but also the underlying principles of how it is created, how it is organised, who accesses it and what it is used for.

In the curriculum, there must be a focus on the process of learning, on how learners engage with and reconstruct knowledge and on content on what is learnt. When we consider knowledge as a finished product, it is organised in the form of information to be 'transferred' to the student's mind. Education would then concern with maintaining and transmitting this storehouse of human knowledge. In this view of knowledge, the learner is conceived as a passive receiver. In the former, learning is dynamic engagement with the world through observing, feeling, reflecting, acting, sharing, thinking, listening, expressing in speech, writing, experiencing, making things, experimenting, reading, discussing and asking questions.

In the Indian way of thinking, there are two types of knowledge—*apara vidya* (lower knowledge) and *para vidya* (higher knowledge). The more we transcend from *apara* to *para vidya* more we become liberated. Lower knowledge is attained by the senses. It is confined to intellectual processes and refers to the highest stores of information. Higher knowledge, on the other hand, crosses the borders of sense knowledge. It crosses the borders of intellectual knowledge. Higher knowledge refers to growing inward, discovering the inner self and inner unity through inner vision and intuition. Indian pedagogy, therefore, insists on the development of faculties of intuition. It calls for a synthesis between the two. In Indian pedagogy, the important word used is *Jyana*–supreme self-knowledge. It talks of various other kinds of knowledge. We have discussed sense knowledge, intellectual knowledge and scientific knowledge. There are also psychological knowledge, philosophical knowledge, ethical knowledge, aesthetic knowledge and knowledge of the world. But according to Indian way of thinking real knowledge is intuitive and supramental. True knowledge leads to liberation from bondage, and in this way, education reaches the level of Yoga.

Conclusion

It can be inferred from the preceding discussion that conceptual clarity of the terms identified in this chapter is quite significant for a practising teacher and teacher educator for planning, organising and implementing the curriculum. Scientific analysis leads us to the various dimensions and aspects of each construct, strategies to be adopted for implementation and specific emphasis to be given to different aspects. In the absence of conceptual clarity, the predetermined objectives cannot be achieved in a desirable manner. Once a teacher understands the concept of teaching, they will improve as a teacher. Similarly, clear comprehension of the scope, nature and specific significance of 'education' will enable the teacher to draw out a comprehensive plan of action for educating in a wider cognitive perspective. Knowledge, however, is the basic concept that needs to be understood by everyone associated with the educational enterprise. National Knowledge Commission, in its Introduction to the 'Report to the Nation', has rightly said that "Knowledge has been recognised as the key driving force in the twenty-first century and India's ability to emerge as a globally competitive player will substantially depend on its knowledge resources".

References

NCERT (2005) **National Curriculum Framework 2005.** New Delhi: NCERT.

Sen Gupta, M. (2005) *Vocational Teacher Preparation* In Vocational Education and Training: Challenges and Strategies Sacheti, Verma & Mehrotra (Ed.) Pandit Sunderlal Sharma Central Institute of Vocational Education, Bhopal.

Sen Gupta, M. (2021) Knowledge and Curriculum, PHI Learning Private Limited, Delhi.

GOI (2009) National Knowledge Commission, Report to the Nation 2006-2009, New Delhi.

22
Revitalising Educational Research

Introduction

Research activities are undertaken by teachers, teacher educators, research fellows and independent researchers for different purposes at different levels within the educational system. Benchmark surveys, achievement surveys, educational surveys, trend reports of research in contemporary educational thrust areas, commissioned research utilising external funding, project-based research, action research leading to improvement in practices and researches by eminent scholars through research fellowships are a few examples in this context. The list can be further extended by including in it Ph.D. and post-doctoral research.

Results of issue-based, project-based and need-based research have been found useful in policymaking, project monitoring, evaluating programmes and administering. Research-based interventions have also been introduced to improve the teaching-learning processes. Many national and state level institutions and NGOs are promoting and are involved in conducting status studies, evaluative studies or tracer studies.

Doing research in one form or the other has been included in the postgraduate curriculum in the universities. This has been done because teaching, training and research are intimately related to each other. Research-oriented students tend to discover and develop new ideas in their search for truth by using systematic enquiry process. In teacher education institutions Master of Education (M.Ed.) degree is the first stage where students are initiated to the educational research methodology.

Later they are required to prepare and submit a dissertation as partial fulfilment of the degree requirements. This initial orientation is followed by M.Phil and Ph.D. degrees. In doing doctoral research, some of the functional constraints like time, resources and coverage get relaxed, leading to the possibility of deeper probes as compared to M.Ed. dissertation. Approach in both these stages is, however, formative.

Students, after going through this process, are now ready to take up in-depth investigations into the realm of educational research. The skills of analysis and interpretation, process of synthesising various elements to form a complete pattern and evaluating or interpreting the obtained conclusions, lead to better understanding of the phenomenon due to better control and rational conduct. Experience, however, shows that in practice, research in education has become a routine activity devoid of the thrill of investigation and discovery. Selection of sample, writing of objectives and deciding variables are all done in a set pattern. Finally, the report is packed within a set of five chapters. These chapters, too, have been further formatted, thereby making the task quite mechanical and manipulative.

It will not be an exaggeration to say that majority of the research in education simply adds to the bulk of stationery rather than to the fund of knowledge. Research findings largely remain within the covers of the thesis or journal and do not percolate into the system. Classrooms and functionaries at the grassroots level, in turn, starve for fresh ideas. The system thus remains devoid of nutrition in the form of research inputs. Research findings due to lack of authenticity, proper validity and reliability remain unacceptable. Most of the time, the real users, viz., teachers in primary and secondary schools, cannot decipher the action points because of research jargon used by researchers that are incomprehensible to them. Dissemination of research results is the weakest link in the whole exercise. Thus, the very purpose of conducting research gets defeated. The system can ill afford to continue with such unproductive, unusable and unauthentic research. It is time that the educationists committed to research take note of the situation and take appropriate action to make educational research truly investigative, responsive and duly acceptable thereby transforming it into a thrilling experience.

Trends and Concerns

A deeper probe into the research reports prepared at M.Ed. and Ph.D. levels will reveal a trend towards using survey methods through self-made or adopted or translated tools and even tools of foreign origin without ascertaining and re-establishing their validity or reliability, or compatibility with the sample or culture. It will be observed that in most cases, data collection and data analysis lack the expected rigour. Meta-analysis or synthesis is very poorly done. Research problems are generated by using catchy words to make them instantly acceptable by the system. Consequently, the researchers hardly probe the contemporary real issues with an open mind and in the spirit of scientific enquiry. Same problems are researched repeatedly using information already available. Due to questionable research processes, results largely go unnoticed. The findings of these research, most of the time, reiterate the known facts. The conscientious teachers and administrators require reliable research results devoid of research jargon. Research results need to be customised and presented in action form for policymakers, administrators and implementers. The system will get a new life only if research shows a new horizon, generates a novel postulate or suggests a promising practice.

"Another discernible trend is towards early completion and getting a degree by any means. Enhancing knowledge or putting one's best to discover the truth is hardly the objective. As a point of fact, research is being directed to selfish short-term goals and not for the sake of bringing improvement in education. Most of the research being conducted in education has the ulterior motive of getting time-bound career advancement, creating for oneself a status of research guide, obtaining membership of various committees or simply to get a degree. In the name of qualitative research, trivial problems are selected, and data are collected by dubious means and unprofessional manner through tools without due regard to their reliability, validity, or suitability" (Sen Gupta, M. 2014). Descriptive survey method, in its most primitive form, is generally used. Quantitative research, more often than not, 'verify' the crudely formulated hypotheses using all sorts of statistical tests without establishing their need or following the underlying assumptions of using these inferential and non-parametric statistics.

A significant fact worth noting in this context is that the big majority of aspirants for jobs as teachers and teacher educators in schools and colleges of education today are composed of girls. The ratio of girls versus boys in a teacher education institution today generally is about 80:20 or may even be 85:15. Therefore, it may be safely inferred that in the times to come, mainly girls will be doing and guiding educational research. They would, therefore, require better and safe mobility, more time to devote, proper guidance and better social motivation and security to be systematic and rigorous in their research endeavour. They would require proper encouragement and research support to improve and sharpen their research competency. Sooner they leave the mindset of fulfilling the immediate requirement, the better for the system.

As with regards to research areas, it is observed that government priority to certain programmes attracts most researchers. In the last decade, we find large number of research on primary education or elementary education since much emphasis was laid in *Sarva Shiksha Abhiyan* (SSA) on universalisation of primary education first and then on the universalisation of elementary education.

Trend reports of researches published in 'Survey of Educational Research' (NCERT, New Delhi), are testimony to the fact that areas like philosophy of education, sociology of education, history of education and economics of education did not get due attention from researchers. Planners and administrators often search for authentic research findings from systemic research and policy research in contemporary social context. Also, one can identify many areas of research concerns such as constructivism vs. behaviourism and need for their synthesis, gender parity for social cohesion, multilingualism as a resource, e-learning, online course offerings, multiple intelligence based curriculum, tracer studies of entrepreneurs, industry-school partnership, generic or soft skills for service sector, identification and nurturance, cruelty on students by teachers, teaching effectiveness and subject preferences of male vs. female teachers, public-private partnership, pedagogical and financial aspects of coaching, tuition by teachers and multiple tuitions by students, sexual abuse of students, studies on ergonomics, privatisation of education without commercialisation, vocational and skill development of children, violence in schools, suicidal tendencies among students and so on, which are not receiving due attention.

Some researchable questions of urgent nature are:

- Why do teachers give corporal punishment? What is their personality profile? Are they trained or untrained? What is their background? Are they male or female?
- Students en masse go for coaching/tuition, why? How successful are these? What strategies lead to success?
- What are the specific needs of rural students and teachers?
- What is examination stress? Why do students suffer from it? How to reduce stress?
- What are the problems that the education system faces because of the decision by many states to introduce English from Class 1? Does learning through English medium affect creativity in Indian students?
- How to bring professionalism into the system? How to lead the system to academic professionalism?
- How to attract talents of both sexes into the profession?
- 'Why do we find the tendency of child abuse in teachers'? 'What are their credentials'?

These and many other contemporary socio-cultural and educational questions deserve serious probing by researchers. Today e-lessons, e-curriculum, e-textbooks, e-evaluation, efficacy of machine-based learning vis-à-vis traditional approach to learning, online teaching, online courses and online training are posing many questions to the researchers.

Need for Good Research

Research stimulates intellectual processes, refines analytical abilities and helps one to move up on the career path. With the strong desire to improve human experience, the researcher positively contributes to the fund of knowledge. A good piece of research reveals the mismatch between expectation and experience. Such revelation may have far-reaching theoretical and/or practical implications. Worthwhile research goes to formulate a new and important problem for investigation. It may also assist in arriving at a new and better solution to an existing problem or developing a constructive way of challenging existing expectations.

As a matter of fact, if a research fails to challenge, it fails to provoke change. In other words, research to be worthwhile should not reinforce prejudices and encourage complacency. Rather it should dare to challenge a significant theory, policy or practice. Research that treats people merely as a means to an end or, in the process, compromises the pursuit of truth by disingenuousness or ineptitude on the part of the researcher can, at best, be termed as bad research.

Research in education is no longer a purely knowledge-seeking activity. Very often, it is also not directed to finding solutions to burning issues in contemporary educational scene. The scene described above is so general all over that notable distinctions or exceptions easily get eclipsed.

Quality Control–An Imperative

Although educational research has quantitatively grown since independence, but one cannot at the same time deny the fact that the research process that has been followed and the resulting research findings have generated scepticism concerning their quality and applicability. Training for educational research at different levels needs to be strengthened. Financial and other incentives need to be woven into the system for research supervisors so that they take the task more seriously. Fixing of accountability of research supervisors at all levels is necessary. Residential programmes of educational research in the universities and other research organisations, strict screening of research scholars, scrutiny of research reports by a specially constituted team and research-based interventions are some other measures in this context. Unfortunately, there are unscrupulous organisations who, instead of doing real professional work, try to make the results sensational, sometimes even at the cost of required rigour in arriving at research results. Most research today are being done by individuals. Group research, mega research, collaborative researches or multidisciplinary researches are a rarity. Recently, however, NCERT under the aegis of ERIC, has got done some useful multicentric studies on pre-service teacher education, decentralised governance and education of SC and ST. Many sponsored projects like on curriculum renewal, textbook writing, teacher education and *Sarva Shiksha Abhiyan* and vocationalisation of secondary education have an inbuilt research component, and funds have been allocated for the same. Formative and summative studies are conducted right from the planning stage of these projects. Continuous monitoring and periodic evaluation provide much-needed feedback for further improvement. UGC, NCERT, ICSSR, Nehru Memorial Fund and many other national organisations have come forward to fund educational research, but worthwhile epoch-making researches are still a far cry.

An important area that is getting dilapidated because of its careless handling is the well-defined area of action research. Today all sorts of research papers are being published in the name of action research. Unfortunately, any research activity is being termed as action research. As a result, it is not serving the very purpose for which it stands. Action research reports too are furnishing the cupboards along with others, which tells a sad commentary.

Revamping Educational Research

The first and foremost requirement in revamping educational research in India is to reorient the teacher educators and research guides through a massive centrally sponsored rigorous orientation programme organised in best-ranking Indian universities where the faculty of education is strong in terms of research-mindedness and facilities. These universities may draw expertise from other research organisations and persons having proven research credentials. Faculties of education in universities should draw priority research areas periodically select, prepare and establish reliability and validity of new tools and techniques; arrange training in using software packages for research analysis and interpretation; organise face-to-face presentation sessions and facilitate a critical look at international research and interaction with foreign and Indian experts through series of researcher's congregations.

Research students in every university must pass through a grill by experts and peers in seminar-like situation at least thrice from registration to submission. Research guides should invariably remain present in such sessions. Every research scholar must publish at least three research papers on their topic before submission and at least two papers after award. Publication of the research and implementable action points in the form of a book should be made mandatory within two years from award of the degree.

Although research degree committees do meet in every university to examine the synopsis submitted, most of the time, it just remains a formality with few suggestions here and there by one identified expert. Instead, seminar cum interview sessions can be 'most rewarding'. The exposure will help students in developing an insight into the problem through extensive discussion and by listening to diverse points of view.

Finally, a suggestion worth mentioning here is that the dissertation at M.Ed. level or theses at Ph.D. and M.Phil. levels should be rated on a three- or five-point scale in terms of its quality, utility, reliability, language, etc. Such grading may work as an incentive to those who achieve better ratings on a set criterion, and this measure may infuse some rigour into the process.

Reference

Sen Gupta, M. (2014) Revamping Educational Research in Universities, *University News*, Sept-Oct, New Delhi.

23

Learning: The Process of Knowledge Creation

Learning: Its Nature

Learning is a natural process. Every child has the potential to learn. It is spontaneous to a human child. Learning is nurtured by a variety of interactions at home, in school and within the community. The child learns through their own experiences as well as from the experiences of others. They acquire these experiences by involving in simple activities and through conversations and numerous interactions with men and material. Experiences thus gained through listening and observing play an important role in cognitive development of the child. Learning gets accelerated in a free environment when the child gets adequate opportunities to explore, experiment, freely assemble and dismantle, commit mistakes and learn from those mistakes. Seen in this perspective, learning is an active, reflective and interactive phenomenon within a social context. Direct involvement of the child in actions extends their understanding. These actions help in developing their intellectual faculties. Development achieved through active participation leads to further creative expression in the form of more enriching activities. Non-availability of adequate opportunities to use various senses during the process of learning, less opportunities for listening and imitating and inadequate practice, particularly at the lower stages, restrict the development of the child's intellect. Actions manifest basically in two ways: one, leading to self-expression and self-improvement and second, to production of things or services useful to the society.

Children learn in a variety of ways. They learn by experiencing, involving in creation of things, manipulating tools and materials, experimenting with different materials and techniques, reading, speaking, asking questions, listening, reflecting, drawing, writing, and expressing themselves through role play, dramatics, debate, dance, music and in many other creative ways.

Pace of learning varies from child to child. Students, most of the time, memorise the given facts when pressed hard by parents or teachers but forget after the examination. Curiously enough, in our system, a child is branded a dullard if they forgets before the examination and an intelligent if they forget after the examination. Learning becomes meaningful only when the child understands the concept and assimilates it such that the effect is observable in behavioural manifestations. Learning, especially in the early years, needs to be characterised by a variety of content, flexibility of transactional modes, involvement in activity and motivation to think, interpret and modify. Interest is created when their established beliefs and sense of imagination are challenged by bringing in novelty in teaching-learning and linking education to the sociocultural milieu.

Opportunities within Stimulating Environment

The child learns better in a stimulating environment. Such an environment gives the child a place of importance, a feeling of higher self-esteem, freedom to explore and experiment, and offers opportunities to derive pleasure and satisfaction through joyful interactions. Every child has a unique personality, their unique way of learning and distinct inner potentialities. Challenging, tolerant, positive and secure school and classroom environments enable the child to learn meaningfully. Fear of physical punishment and ridicule restricts the possibilities of learning and may even give rise to negative attitudes.

The child, by nature, is active. An infant, so long as it is awake, throws its hands or feet, cries, laughs or moves its eyeballs. It is never still. But no sooner the same child enters the premises of a preschool, they are made to put their finger on the lips', sit firmly and calmly without any movement and is expected to listen to the unidirectional instructions of the teacher. In other words, the school deliberately and systematically makes the child inactive or passive. In the name of discipline and strict control over students, we are, in fact, going against the very nature of the child. Human child is self-motivated to learn and has a spectacular capability of self-learning. But the process gets stultified due to faulty teaching strategies, the absence of enriching opportunities and an authoritative classroom environment. Opportunities for developing abstract thinking, to search for meanings and analogies, situations to form and understand concepts and doing constructive activities have a significant role in augmenting purposive learning.

Process of Knowledge Construction

In the process of enabling the child to create knowledge, the teacher has a pivotal role to play. It is essential for the teacher to distinguish between knowledge and information. Mere transfer of information cannot be termed as imparting education. Knowledge or education is not a physical entity that can be transferred and handed over to the child. Education, in effect, is the process of creating and constructing knowledge by the child. The urge to learn and efforts of the child in that direction become very important. The job of the teacher is to understand the nature of the child, assess the relevance and significance of the content and devise opportunities wherein the child can express and interact through a variety of media, experiment with a variety of tools, materials and techniques and meaningfully explore the natural and social environment. Students will be able to experience the joy of knowledge and thrill of understanding only when critical and creative thinking and insight and intuition are given due importance in the process of teaching and learning. Participation in well-planned and mutually executed projects helps in the construction of knowledge.

It is necessary to bring a change in the commonly held viewpoint that children are the receivers of knowledge and that textbooks are the source of knowledge. Creating knowledge through personal involvement and first-hand experience requires to be duly recognised. Wherever possible, simulated situations and tasks should be devised to solve problems or work online with the help of latest digital technology. Parents need to be educated and examinations suitably reformed to combat the trend of reading each page of the textbook in the class and learning by rote. Identified portions of the syllabus can be learnt by self-study, mutual discussion in smaller groups or through project work and assignment. In a similar manner, change may be brought about in the general approach of the parents regarding the future of their children. Unnecessary pressure on them to compete and excel in every field of life, irrespective of their specific capabilities or interests, needs to be rationalised. The stress should rather be on helping them in giving their best in whatever they do in accordance with their capabilities.

Today opportunities have multiplied to such an extent that every child has something to choose from as per his or her inclinations and reach the desired financial landmark without sacrificing individual talents. Artificial adjustment in predetermined grooves, as per the whims of the parents, needs to be discouraged at any cost. The focus should be on nurturing creativity, encouraging innovativeness and developing entrepreneurship. The voice of the child, their day-to-day experiences, viewpoints, new or unusual ideas and richness of interactions should be encouraged at home and in the process of teaching and learning. Situations are to be created, and opportunities given for taking the initiative, thinking afresh on existing problems, asking questions, raising doubts, evaluating and judging within and outside the class. Competition and cooperation need to be balanced for reducing stress and developing mutual understanding.

Role of the Teacher

In today's perspective, a teacher cannot be seen as an instrument of disbursing information. The teacher can no longer continue to transfer the accumulated information through lectures or by reading from textbooks.

The preceding description may become clear and comprehensible by citing one or two examples from classroom teaching-learning situations. In one rural primary school, the teacher was teaching a general science lesson on 'living and non-living things'. He wrote names of three living and three non-living things on the blackboard. He then asked the children to note them down on their notebooks. They were then instructed to learn them by heart for reproducing the same later in the examination. This is an example of transfer of information by the teacher devoid of any possibility of knowledge creation by the students. Instead, if the teacher had explained the characteristics of living and non-living things, presented analogies, distinguished them with examples and then asked the children to look around in the village and make their own lists of the two types, it would have opened a process of discussion with peers and with other knowledgeable persons. Children would apply the criteria, compare their findings, clarify their doubts and thus understand the phenomenon by their own efforts.

It has often been noticed that teachers, in general, do not allow students to ask questions simply to hide their own ignorance or to avoid the trouble of referring to advanced books. For example, while teaching 'photosynthesis' in a science classroom, the teacher defines the term and dictates the process to be noted and memorised by the students. This path of least resistance is chosen because they feel threatened by the child's probable questions such as how does a plant prepare its food although its leaves are not green but red in colour or how does a plant survive even when it does not have even a single leaf for months together. As a matter of fact, such questions do arise in the minds of the children based on their observations, but the teacher tends to curb their curiosity to have a smooth sailing in the classroom and to hide their own ignorance. It is useful to realise that the teacher also learns in the process of teaching. With little efforts many doubts get cleared. In a reflective teaching environment, students and teachers ultimately reach the realm of unknown together, thereby sowing the seeds of invention and innovation.

The teachers, whether urban or rural, because of obvious reasons, neither find time nor have an inner urge to go deeper into the phenomenon. They consider it easier to put forward a dominating self-image so that children desist from asking questions out of fear or driven by a feeling of possible humiliation before their classmates. The teacher hardly appreciates the fact that when children bring their personal or collective experiences into the classroom and thereby debatable issues come to surface, the situation presents a challenging opportunity requiring collective efforts to resolve them in a cooperative manner. It is only then that new ideas emerge, unusual solutions are suggested and the teacher leads the learner in the quest for further knowledge.

Classroom Climate

Free and secure classroom climate where ideas are generated, problem-solving capabilities are nurtured and the voice of the child is heard can only ensure creation of new knowledge, however insignificant it may be. In a heterogeneous classroom where children of varying abilities, aptitudes and interests learn together, any single method is bound to fail to address the varying needs. It would call for using a variety of methods to suit the varying needs of children. Freedom to enquire, opportunities to raise doubts, mutual learning and reflective teaching can make education to move away from preparing dignified clerks and usher in a new classroom environment dominated by independence, creativity, self-discipline, innovativeness and self-control. Children need to be encouraged to learn from many unconventional/digital sources besides textbooks.

Unfortunately, the process of education even today is limited to presenting the traditionally drafted and nicely written lesson plans verbatim, which often are nothing but mirror images of textbook pages. Both teachers and administrators are primarily concerned with the marks obtained by students by reproducing the known in the examinations. Thus, there is hardly any motivation for allowing children to probe into the unknown on their own. The usual practice of drawing up lesson plans mechanically and presenting in a routine manner in the classroom needs to be seriously reviewed if credibility of the system has to remain intact in the eyes of the students and the community. Teachers should be encouraged to plan their lessons meticulously, keeping in view the previous and present knowledge of the child, ensuring spontaneous active participation of the child, and extending the knowledge base beyond the textbook. This will enable children to reflect, innovate and indulge in higher-order thinking.

Children tend to judge situations and evaluate their own needs in their own peculiar way. Their experiences and feelings must be respected during classroom transactions. Their cognitive abilities should be so developed that they can debate and discuss, invent, and innovate freely and with conviction without being influenced by any preconceived notions. They should develop courage to differ, confidence to argue and ultimately arrive at a negotiated but just settlement. In the globalised market economy decision-making, entrepreneurship and negotiation skills are considered essential for progress and success.

Children need to be acquainted with the various forms of media and their potentialities. Interaction with media helps in knowledge creation by relating the information with day-to-day realities of life. Purposive processing of information, categorising them for better comprehension and developing capability to use them for one's own objectives transform the undigested information into assimilated knowledge.

Assessment and Evaluation

Evaluation, instead of simply testing the memory, should give due weightage to other equally important aspects of child development like ability to take initiative, trying new ways of solving a problem, generation of useful ideas, originality in thinking and expression, interpretation of data and taking data-based decisions. In the present-day examination-driven system, it is assumed that knowledge is always created by 'experts' and the child is only expected to receive and memorise it. This develops in the child a trend towards collecting information from secondary sources and learning them by rote without understanding their implications. Therefore, they are not able to enjoy cognitive self-introspection, joy of discovery and inherent flexibility in knowledge creation. As a result, even after completion of elementary education, they do not develop the capability of expressing themselves freely and discerning meaning from the learning experiences or appreciating them in the right perspective.

Conclusion

Every child has the capacity to learn and is endowed with one or the other talent that needs to be identified and nurtured. Each child needs to be motivated and encouraged to perform even better and thus move forward towards the goal of excellence. Classroom teaching-learning becomes relevant and understanding of concepts become easy when the children are able to appreciate the implications of classroom instructions and can relate them to real-life situations. Discussion in smaller groups, participatory development of the lesson, involving children in decision-making and allowing them to think, find and discover can be some useful strategies in this context. Use of local resources, utilising multiple media, referring to journals and reference books, and exemplifying through folk tales, role play, dramatics, seminars and group discussions have tremendous potentialities. These develop the imagination, listening skills, a culture of reading and self-study. Imagination and originality are the keywords in the present-day context. A balanced development of competition and cooperation is desirable. Teaching-learning, thus, is a multidimensional and complex process, which has the capability of providing joy and satisfaction to the child. Once the child feels the joy and imbibes an urge to learn more, he sets out to a mission towards new and unknown horizons, which in the long run opens up newer possibilities to further the cause of the welfare of the larger community.

24

Activity-based Cognitive Development

Cognitive development of a child during their first two years is mainly through sensory experiences derived from motor activities. The child obtains environmental information through its senses and reflexes. It gets attracted to changes in sounds, movements and colours in the surrounding. In the early years, the child visually follows the objects and looks for a hidden object at the place where it was earlier. It begins to understand cause and effect relationships. For example, the child relates its own crying to catching mother's attention and movement of a toy to some sort of sound production.

Close to two years, the development of the process of imagination begins. The child indulges in games involving acting or pretending. It starts using symbols for things or people. For instance, it uses a box as a bed or for a table. The child may move a toy on a railing pretending it to be a train. In its playful way, the child innocently imitates others. For example, it pretends to put its doll to sleep just like its mother does, or imitates a dog's movements and the way it barks. In a similar manner, the child starts learning language skills. It is a common observation that children nicely imitate advertisements shown on TV.

As the child develops imagination and language skills, it begins recognising the objects and figures shown in a picture or scenery. Based on experience, it understands that certain incidents take place periodically at regular intervals, like day and night. In a similar manner, by experiencing morning, evening and night, the child gradually begins to develop the notion of time. During this period, itself, the child starts developing pre-number concepts. It now begins to understand the concepts of big-small, more-less, light-heavy and the like. Understanding of number also follows by relating to one nose, two eyes, two ears, one tongue, five fingers and so on. Subsequently, this lays the foundation of the processes of addition and subtraction.

Around the age of six, the child is able to categorise or differentiate things according to colour, shape and size. It can recognise beads of different colours, say red, green and blue and thus is able to separate them accordingly. Similarly, it can select and place separately grains, pulses or seeds. Its thinking now becomes more organised and systematic. These very changes in thinking and organisation, along with their ability to classify and solve problems, become stepping stones to further cognitive development. These days cognitive development is very much influenced by the manipulation of electronic gadgets.

The sequential development of cognitive capacities in children, described by Jean Piaget, lays much stress on the richness of a child's interactions with the immediate environment. According to Piaget, every normal child by birth has the ability of learning and understanding. It also has a natural tendency of adjusting with the environment. Being in continuous contact with the environment, it acclimatises with its nature and develops the ability to face the environmental changes efficiently. Just as the body derives nutrition by assimilating the food, similarly cognitive or intellectual development draws its nutrition from interaction with environmental stimulations.

Cognitive Skills and their Stimulation

Memory:

All human beings are able to remember facts, names and other pieces of information with the help of their memory. Remembering and recognising are its two facets. In order to remember the facts and figures for a longer duration, continuous practice and repetition are important. Use of more senses in the process of learning is found helpful in remembering. It is always advisable to teach children through the medium of manipulative activities since many senses get involved in the process of doing. The five senses of seeing, feeling, touching, listening and tasting play important roles in the improvement of memory. The process of memory gets promoted by using the skills of analogy and comparing or contrasting. Also, when the child gets interested in any subject its ability to remember that subject matter content increases.

In order to develop the interest of children and to maintain their concentration towards a particular content, it is essential to keep them active during the process of learning. Given information will be meaningful to the children only when it is linked to their own needs or with the immediate environment. Content presented within a lesson should be easy to comprehend, and those parts which children are likely to forget should be revised often. Loud reading is found useful in enhancing memory. Memory is the mother of imagination, creativity, reasoning and meaning.

Thinking, Reasoning and Problem-Solving

In the thinking process, sensory experiences act as raw materials. Information obtained through the senses is organised based on their unique perception. Cognitive development in children is a slow and long process. It depends on many other factors such as social, emotional and physical development. Teachers should encourage and let children take small and easy decisions themselves. For example, which dress to wear and when, which doll or toy to pick up for play and which food items to select for lunch or dinner.

In the process of developing reasoning, children consider every aspect of a suggestion, activity or proposal and try to arrive at the best possible solution. The teacher will pose common problems related to different situations from day-to-day life and motivate them to find their solutions. If need be, they may be given hints here and there. Sensory stimulation for cognitive development not only helps in memorising but also assists in the development of many cognitive skills like observation, classification, sequential thinking, problem-solving and reasoning. Children acquire digital literacy through trial and error, imitation and practice. They enjoy solving puzzles and problems.

Role of Teachers

In order to ensure the proper development of cognitive capacities in children, it is important that children are allowed to manipulate objects and materials freely. It should always be possible for them to meet and talk to friends and teachers. They should be given enough opportunities to participate in a variety of activities. Free thinking needs to be encouraged in children to develop their creativity. Day-to-day problems will be presented to them in such a way that they can judge these from all possible angles before suggesting a possible solution. Teachers should never provide a readymade solution to problems; rather, they need to help students in reaching a satisfactory solution on their own. Teachers should never discourage or ridicule a child if they are unable to do work as directed. The teacher should always encourage children to ask questions. Every child has a unique personality. Each one is different from the others. Everyone thinks differently and accomplishes a work differently, and hence the teacher should respect these individual differences.

Activities for Cognitive Development

To assist in cognitive development by sensory stimulation, it is useful to involve children in group activities under the direction of teachers. Following are some exemplary activities that can easily be organised by teachers:

Matching similar objects: In this activity, there will be two sets of cards. In one set, there will be cards bearing pictures of fruits like mango, guava and grapes, while the other set of cards will bear pictures of transport facilities like buses, aeroplanes, railway trains and boats. Both these sets of cards will be thoroughly mixed. Now children will be asked to identify and collect cards bearing pictures of fruits and make a set and then identify cards bearing pictures of transport facilities and make another set.

Similar activities can be done with cards bearing pictures of vegetables, leaves, flowers, pets, colours, coins and so on.

Identifying the dissimilar one: Cut four 25x5 cm strips from a drawing sheet. On a strip, make or paste five pictures consisting of four frogs and one horse's head. Similarly, on another strip, there will be four lion's heads and one of bird. The third strip will have pictures of four apples and one banana. The fourth strip can have pictures of four mangoes and one apple. The position of the dissimilar object can vary in each strip.

Let children sit in a semi-circular form. Show them each strip one by one. Let them identify the object that is different or dissimilar from others. Encourage those who give right answers.

Identifying floating/sinking or light/heavy objects: Fill a tub with water. Children will collect some objects like a piece of paper, an iron nail, a small stone, a leaf, a pin, a bird's feather, etc. They will place the objects one by one in water and find out those that sink and those that float. They will infer that those things which are heavy will sink and things which are light will float on the surface of the water.

Classification: In order to develop in children, the ability to classify, they may do the following activities:

- Classifying the given cards in terms of their shape like circular, triangular, rectangular and elliptical
- Identifying and categorising things in terms of their shape, for example, cards bearing pictures of circular things like plate, saucer, *roti, chakla,* bangle and wheel of a bicycle; triangular things like triangular *paratha, samosa,* seat of a bicycle and triangular cap and rectangular things like book, table, window, door and almirah
- Categorising things in terms of colours like red, yellow, blue and green
- Identifying and keeping separately the leaves of mango, papya, neem, banana, guava, pumpkin, etc.
- Classifying different vegetables
- Identifying and classifying seeds of tamarind, pumpkin, plum, bitter gourd, watermelon, etc.
- Correlating the pairs of lock–key, shoe–socks, pant–shirt, racket–shuttle cork, tie–clip, hockey-stick–ball, etc.

Identifying the deficiencies by observing given pictures:

For this activity, flashcards will be prepared with pictures of a man, scooter, bicycle, car, fan, etc., with a deficiency in each. For example, a hand missing in a man's picture, one wheel missing from a scooter, one peddle missing in a bicycle, an ear missing from a horse's picture and the player having shoes only in one foot.

Children will find out the missing thing or part. This joyful activity will sharpen their observation skill.

Teachers, in a similar manner, can devise and include many more activities that promote imagination and assist in the development of cognitive skills. Ensuring active participation of children, these activities can be made interesting and educative. Activities should be so contrived that they activate the children's senses and nurture their sensitivities.

Through such activities, children will develop skills of working in groups, carrying out instructions and carefully storing the cards. Simultaneously this will enhance their cognitive development and their vocabulary will also be enriched.

25

Teaching Approach for PG Classes

Introduction

Teaching is always contextual in nature. It is intimately related to learning, the learner, learning environment and the stipulated learning goals. It can neither be singularly defined for all times to come nor can it be applied to all types of students or, for that matter, all stages of education uniformly. As we move upwards from lower to higher stages of education, teaching undergoes qualitative change in favour of critical and analytical thinking, mutual discussions and independent study, peer presentations and abstract thinking. However, teaching gains relevance only when it results in learning through the active involvement of the learners. It is only through active participation that learning becomes lasting. In order to ensure or facilitate learning, the teacher has to take into consideration the learner's previous experiences, his readiness to learn and motivation–both intrinsic and extrinsic. Teaching becomes effective when it is altered, adjusted or fine-tuned, keeping in view the needs of the learners. Other factors affecting the quality of teaching in an institutional perspective are the attitude of the Principal and other colleagues, cooperation of supporting staff, availability of infrastructural facilities, incentives for progressive improvement, the evaluation system and the nature of examination.

Teaching Approach

Psychology of the learner and their developmental stage, along with the nature of content, decide the methods of teaching to be used. For example, at the earlier stages of schooling it becomes imperative to concretise the abstract ideas by arranging demonstrations, using models and other teaching aids, and making use of audio, video or other projective techniques. But at the undergraduate and postgraduate levels, the method frequently adopted by an average teacher is either lecture or lecture cum discussion. Students are required to put in effort to prepare their notes by using available print and non-print resources. At this advanced stage, learners are more autonomous. Given the right references, they prefer self-study, like to interact with peers and are career oriented. In order to promote independent thinking, healthy competitive spirit and an urge to excel, the teaching approach should focus on more discussion and debate rather than spoon-feeding.

In other words, the approach to be followed in case of post-graduate professional courses have to be entirely different. For example, M.Ed. is a postgraduate professional course. Students joining this course are adults. They are self-motivated and would prefer to learn by their own efforts. Hence, a method which provides scope for self-learning, self-presentation and peer discussion enthuses them to engage actively in the process of learning. They eagerly contribute by collecting information, preparing discussion papers or participating in the process of learning.

As we know M.Ed. is a professional course to prepare teacher educators. This would include developing professional competence, infusing a sense of conviction and commitment, and ensuring their mastery in methodological and pedagogical issues. In order to professionalise the process of teaching-learning, the teacher educator himself or herself has to first set an example in conducting and managing information and communication technology-based classrooms, taking research and data-based decisions and providing value-based working leadership. The student at M.Ed. level should be inspired to read more, refer encyclopaedias and dictionaries, go to original sources to clarify their concepts and broaden their mental horizons by apprising themselves with the latest developments at national and international levels. An unending quest for knowledge is essential to keep oneself abreast of new concepts, new interpretations and newer results of contemporary research.

Experiment Conducted

It will not be out of place to elaborate this point by citing an experiment done by the author with M.Ed. students while teaching the paper on 'Educational and Vocational Guidance'. The experiment went on as follows:

1. To begin with, the author thoroughly analysed the syllabus to arrive at specific topics or issues related to each unit.
2. The class was then divided into groups. Each group consisting of two students was assigned either one or two topics/issues depending upon their motivation and liking. Thus, all the topics/issues identified earlier were distributed almost uniformly to the class.
3. The students were given required information about available resources like related books, library references and internet locations. They were asked to study, prepare notes, exchange notes, if necessary and ultimately present a comprehensive paper on the assigned topic/issue.
4. The author simultaneously consulted the best of libraries. By browsing latest literature, encyclopaedia and other classical sources, he made detailed notes on each topic covering all the topics/issues. The focus was on latest and accurate information presented in a lucid manner.
5. Subsequently, in a classroom situation, each group presented their paper with their own analysis and interpretation. All others listened and discussed the paper as per their own knowledge of the topic. The author participated in the discussions along with students to clarify doubts or to straighten any differences of opinion.

6. Finally, the author presented his own notes on the topic/issue explaining difficult concepts and filling the gaps observed in the presentations.
7. This process continued for all the topics/issues, thus covering the full syllabus.

It is highly satisfying to report that the experiment went on successfully for the whole year. Students participated wholeheartedly in presentations and the discussions that followed. Thus, instead of covering the syllabus by giving lectures on each topic, students themselves prepared papers, presented, discussed and made note of the latest developments and tips given by the teacher educator. It is satisfying to report that in the end, every student passed with very good marks in the university examination. It may, therefore, be inferred that to students who are already postgraduates, every piece of content need not be presented in lecture mode. Much of the syllabus can be covered with their active cooperation and participation using variety of strategies such as discussion in groups, peer learning, assignments, seminars, panel discussion, team teaching, brainstorming, power point presentations and videos and ICT enabled short presentations. The idea is to go beyond the lecture method and also beyond the prescribed textbooks. It was observed that discussion on each topic was extremely useful and enriching. In the process, they clarified their doubts and newer dimensions emerged on many issues. The innovative methodology created much interest among students.

Inference

The experience thus gained suggested that while teaching M.Ed. classes traditional lecture method is neither suitable nor desirable. This is because at this stage the intention is not simply to transact and transfer the content but to develop in students an insight into the issues, an analytical and situational approach to understanding and to awaken their *vivek,* i.e., their ability to judge, to evaluate and to distinguish between good and bad, useful and superficial and between fact and farce.

In other words, the teacher must familiarise themselves about the objectives and outcomes of learning at a particular stage of education. As indicated earlier, M.Ed. students are distinctly different as they are mature and have access to large learning resources. They know how to process and use the available information to their advantage. What they probably require is imaginative and productive application of this information. They may want to understand the results of unusual combinations and implications of creatively synthesised and analysed information, thereby judging the appropriateness of events, strategies or decisions. Practical situations, interesting anecdotes, open-ended questions on current problematic issues, interpretation of texts and elaboration of ideas are some other apt examples to be considered by concerned teachers in this context.

While much has been discussed about teaching in lower classes, not much change is visible in real classroom transactional strategies. This is probably because the nature of teacher training in teacher education institutions is largely theoretical. No role models or living examples of demonstrative classroom strategies have practically been presented before the 'would-be teachers' by the teacher educators in their own classroom transactions. Experiences show that the student of M.Ed. despite holding an additional PG degree, seldom displays command over any one language. In-depth understanding of a phenomenon, certain amount of commitment towards excellence, a rational way of approaching and solving problems, analysing an issue from its philosophical or sociological perspective and a quest for knowledge and quality are some traits that one expects from a student who has obtained a postgraduate degree in any subject. But teaching-learning being *Shruti-Smriti* based, the critical faculties of mind remain largely untapped. This perhaps calls for a wider discussion within the teaching community in higher education as to how PG teaching-learning can be made research-based with stress on 'doing' and 'performing' rather than simply 'telling' and 'knowing'.

Conclusion

The preceding discussion makes it amply clear that the teaching methodology at M.Ed. level needs to be suitably varied and transformed, keeping in view the product that is being prepared and the role they are expected to play in their later life. The individuals and their characteristics, the professional requirements of a teacher/teacher educator, the subject matter content to be transacted and the attitudes and values to be inculcated will ultimately determine the methodology of teaching to be adopted. It is essential to understand that in their later working life, a trained person behaves within the same training framework through which they have passed during their training period. Rarely new strategies are adopted, or different combinations are tried by individuals. Therefore, during the M.Ed. training period, each student must frequently handle the latest technological aids and make live presentations to B.Ed. students, actively participate in seminars or symposiums, observe pupil teachers teaching in a class, physically organise various cultural events and engage in games and sports activities. The idea is to produce henceforth such teacher educators who shun the word 'should' and start doing what they normally preach. From preachers they have to emerge as role models to change the face of present-day classroom transactions and wipe out passive listening on the part of the students. The children construct their own knowledge. Let the teacher educator set an example before the teachers and demonstrate how to make teaching not only interesting and informative but also ensuring participation of the children in knowledge-making, active thinking and creative problem-solving by bringing into practice a much-emphasised variety in teaching methodology.

26

Competency-Based Learning: A Policy Imperative

The emergence of competency-based learning may be termed as an innovative learning initiative in which learners are expected to demonstrate their learned knowledge, skills and attainment of required personal and social qualities in order to achieve specific predetermined competencies. This type of learning focuses on learning outcomes and real-world performance. Learners are given multiple opportunities to attain mastery in a competency. In this process, they are given continuous feedback by the teachers. Being learner-focused and learner-driven, competency-based learning allows different learners in a course to move at varying paces. The assessment of learners in attaining these competencies is done continuously at different points during the course. Based on the performance of the learner on specific competency, the teacher revises instructional strategies accordingly. This is done till he attains mastery level. Mastery level of a competency depends on the nature of the subject matter and the criteria fixed for its attainment. A variety of assessment methods are to be used for assessing the programme-level competencies. Portfolios are often used as an instrument in this context.

Competency and its Significance

A combination of knowledge, skills and socio-personal attributes possessed by a person is generally termed competency. A person performing a job requires certain specific competencies to efficiently accomplish the tasks or professional practices. One is said to be competent in a task when they apply their abilities and use their personality traits in appropriate but consistent manner to achieve the desired performance level. Competencies are multidimensional in nature. These are linked to the desired level of performance in a job. Competencies are to be stated in a way that these are observable and measurable so that these can be comprehensibly assessed. The desired competencies, both general and specific, can be nurtured and developed in individuals to reinforce their competitive advantages. Competencies, when effectively applied, produce a successful performance in each function or activity.

The ability of a person to rightly identify and adequately acquire the required set of functional as well as behavioural competencies proves to be a key differentiator for his future success. The behavioural competencies help in acquiring and applying the functional competencies more effectively by improving interpersonal relationships and personal efficiency. Competency, in addition, comprises aspects of self-concept, self-esteem, social motives and ways of thinking, feeling and doing.

As said earlier, a person to be successful requires desired technical competencies essential to perform a given job. These competencies enable efficient handling of his role in a specialised department. For example, a person involved in management requires competencies of planning, organising and implementing events and programmes. They in addition require qualities of leadership and teamwork to efficiently organise and implement them within the organisation. In this process, they obtain cooperation by motivating the team members for optimum efficiency. However, Sen Gupta (2017) opined that "At times, it is found that the specialised technical skills associated with different (work) roles are considered less important by the employer than the soft skills that are transferable between different jobs and different employment sectors. They instead prefer to hire those candidates who have well-honed set of soft or employability skills". Incidentally, these employability skills include ease in working as a team member, ability to solve problems, taking part in group discussions, dealing with difficult colleagues, readiness to go for entrepreneurial ventures, negotiating deals successfully, ability to manage time, stress, or conflict and so on.

Competency-Based Learning

The present-day curriculum is discipline or subject centred. Its classroom transaction is mainly teacher centred. In a face-to-face situation, the teacher remains active before and during teaching, whereas students largely remain passive. However, this activeness is limited to transferring knowledge created by others. In a discipline-centred curriculum, the content organisation is historical rather than future oriented. It is academically neutral. As opposed to this, learning in a competency-based curriculum focuses on developing specific competencies in a maximum number of learners. In order to see that the desired competency is developed to a particular extent, the teacher is ready to offer more time and different resources, try a variety of approaches and provide content from various points of view. Stress is also on self-paced learning and independent study. Competency-based curriculum allows the learners to focus on one competency at a time. It constitutes a small component of a larger learning goal. Once the student masters the individual competency and has been evaluated on it, he moves on to other competencies. In this manner, after mastering initial competencies, the learner learns higher or more complex competencies to a degree of mastery.

At this juncture, it will be useful to recollect NPE 2020 policy statement, where it states, "While learning by rote can be beneficial in specific contexts, pedagogy must evolve to make education more experiential, holistic, integrated, discovery-oriented, learner-centred, discussion-based, flexible, and, of course, enjoyable". The school curriculum, therefore, must devise ways and means to impart experiential learning and develop in students the right kind of knowledge, skills, attitudes and values in order to enable them to face successfully the challenges posed by the rapid scientific advancements and technological developments. This will help them to adequately face and nicely adjust to new job-related demands and changing socio-economic conditions.

Competency-based learning, as a matter of principle, is child centred. It nicely adapts to the changing needs of learners, teachers and society. In this type of curriculum, learning situations, activities and environments are so selected that the learners get ample opportunities to acquire and apply their attained knowledge, skills and attitudes in day-to-day problem situations. To put it in simple language, it focuses on what the learners will be expected to do or carry out later in life, in higher education or in their careers. It does not simply involve what they are expected to know by way of studying different subjects.

A distinctive feature of competency-based learning is that whenever there is any deficiency, it helps the learner by giving remedial instruction, additional information, more time to practice or by providing academic support in the form of better and varied resources. This is done till the learner achieves the desired level of competency to satisfy the expected standards. The goal here is to ensure that more students learn what they are expected to learn by making the time flexible and through additional instruction or by providing alternative resources. In this way, it is more effective than traditional approaches where students are evaluated in their terminal behaviour primarily to ascertain their status and certify.

Competency-based learning gives an option to the learner to even skip a learning module entirely, provided by virtue of their prior learning, they can demonstrate that they have already acquired mastery over it (Sen Gupta, 2021). Due to flexibility in time and resources, learners can practice and refine as much as they like and then move rapidly to other skills. In other words, competency-based learning aims at mastery of competencies by every individual.

Developing Competency-Based Curriculum

Developing a competency-based curriculum requires the identification of the required set of content-based competencies in functional terms fortified by related behavioural competencies. This is done based on a thorough job analysis and task analysis. Competencies are stated as statements that describe the characteristics expected to be demonstrated by a graduating learner. The statement indicates the learner's capacity to perform and function independently in an academic, vocational, or professional practice situation. Each competency integrates into itself the application of learned information, performance of skills and display of personal qualities such as desired attitudes and values essential to do a job efficiently and effectively. In practice, however, several courses usually collectively assist in the attainment of each competency.

Competency-based curriculum preparation involves bringing together a group of subject experts, practitioners from the field and curriculum experts. They, in close collaboration, develop the said curriculum. In the process of developing a competency-based curriculum, the first task is to identify the required set of functional competencies along with the desired behavioural competencies. These are identified based on systematic analysis of the job into tasks to be performed. Each task is then analysed to identify the functional competencies in terms of knowledge, skills and personality traits. Functional competencies are those competencies which are required to perform a particular function successfully. These include specific knowledge and their application, i.e., skills required to perform the specified tasks or functions. These are fortified by behavioural competencies, which help one to improve one's own effectiveness through better intra- and interpersonal relationships.

Each course syllabus includes course goals. These goals are then specified into specific course objectives. With a view to assess the extent of achievement by a student, these objectives are written using precise language in measurable terms. Successful attainment of all course objectives by a student indicates their mastery.

Development of competency-based curriculum follows the following steps.

The first step consists of identifying the minimum characteristics that an ideal graduate learner is expected to possess in order to successfully practice his higher education initiatives or be successful in his chosen vocation or profession. In other words, the curriculum developer is required to identify specific learning outcomes in terms of performance and behaviour, including the appropriate criterion level to be used in evaluating achievement. This is followed by listing down of necessary knowledge, skills and attitudes or values to be imbibed by the individual for the attainment of each competency thus identified. It is, however, advisable to indicate the methods of assessing the performance in relation to each competency. In order to acquire these competencies necessary course content, course outlines in the form of course units are arranged in a particular sequence. Practical exercises and other related activities may also be specified that will be helpful in attaining the competencies and later in the assessment. At every successive stage, the curriculum would specify the required level of performance to be achieved. These motivate the learners to further practice and demonstrate competency. The curriculum also presents a plan for remediation in case the learner is unable to attain the competency to the desired mastery level.

Competency-based Assessment

While delivering a competency-based curriculum, it is imperative to ascertain that students have gained knowledge, are able to apply and execute that knowledge, the skills and abilities to a level desired by the industry. For the assessment of competency, it is crucial to connect the identified knowledge, skills, and attitudes in a structured manner. While assessing competency, it is essential to address questions like 'have the learners acquired the desired competencies on completion of the course? 'Was the acquisition of the competencies by the learners a result of the inputs provided in the programme?'

NEP 2020 mentioned that "The aim of assessment in the culture of our schooling system will shift from one that primarily tests rote memorisation skills to one that is more formative, is more competency-based, promotes learning and development for our students, and tests higher-order skills, such as analysis, critical thinking, and conceptual clarity". In this context, it is useful to understand that a curriculum founded on developing specified competencies in learners up to a particular mastery level is amenable to a very different kind of assessment scheme.

In order to ascertain the successful attainment of competency by the learner, it is essential to diagnose his status at the completion of each stage. Thus, the assessment of the extent of competencies attained by the students has to be continuous and ongoing rather than being a one-time affair. With the help of such formative diagnostic testing, it would be known whether the learner requires more time, more personalised attention and further inputs or requires altogether different learning opportunities to reach the expected competency level. The development of competencies being incremental in nature, the teacher helps the learner not only to acquire the competency but also to improve upon the competencies.

It is important to appreciate that any discrete assessment of a single aspect will be counterproductive. This is because competency assessment is comprehensive and involves all three domains–cognitive, psycho-motor and affective. Systematic observation and expert subjective judgment play an important part in such assessments. This implies that summative or year-end examination is not suitable for competency assessment. In spite of the subjectivity involved, the validity of the assessment of competencies can be improved by involving multiple assessors, a greater number of assessments and assessment of different tasks.

Conclusion

From this account, it may be concluded that while subject-centred education is time bound and focuses on knowledge only, competency-based learning integrates within itself the three aspects of a child's growth, namely knowledge, skills, and personality traits like attitude and values. Workforce in the knowledge age is expected to know their job well, do each task efficiently, must have the will and positive attitude and be ready to adapt as per changing demands. Any attempt to see them in isolation will defeat the very purpose of education.

Competency-based learning is focused on the complex outcomes of a learning process rather than simply focusing on the subject matter content. These outcomes of the learning process relate not only to the learner's knowledge but also the skills acquired and the attitudes developed. The competency-based curriculum, in addition, provides academic support in the form of better and varied resources till the learner achieves the desired level of competency to satisfy the expected standards.

Competency-based teaching is much more than just a different style of teaching. This is because competency-based education follows an outcome-based approach. It is, as a matter of fact, a definite improvement over the present-day time-bound education because, in this curriculum, the outcome is specifically defined in terms of the level of competency to be achieved.

References

Government of India (2020) *National Education Policy.* Ministry of Human Resource Development, New Delhi.

NCERT, (2005) *National Curriculum Framework 2005.* New Delhi.

Sen Gupta, M. (2017) *Skills for Employability – A Handbook.* New Delhi: Innovative Publication.

27

Developing Thinking in Children

Introduction

Thinking, reasoning and problem-solving are exclusive characteristics of human beings. Human thought or thinking can be described as the mental process through which the concerned person forms mental associations and models of the material world. In the process of thinking, information obtained is purposely manipulated either to solve a specific problem or to take certain decisions.

The thinking process of reasoning is done in a logical way in order to arrive at a conclusion or to form a judgment. In other words, it is the ability of the mind to think and understand things in a logical way. The faculty of intellect that relates to reason or reasoning is considered the ultimate source of knowledge by rationalists. Rationalists assume that knowledge is obtained by reasoning. Through persistent reasoning, they try to understand the truths about reality. Reason is considered as an important source because through reasoning one can deduce truth from existing knowledge. Truth can also be reached by discovering, taking recourse to pure reason, going from cause to effect or from assumption to discovery of necessary truths. Knowledge based on reasoning can be inferred either through inductive reasoning or by deductive reasoning.

Thinking Skills

There are basically two types of thinking skills. These are convergent thinking skills and divergent thinking skills. While critical thinking is an important component of convergent thinking skills, creative/lateral thinking falls within the purview of divergent thinking skills. The processes of thinking and reasoning play an important role in decision-making and problem-solving. These thinking skills do not function in isolation rather, they supplement and complement each other. However, each may be distinguished by their specific characteristics.

Critical Thinking

Critical thinking may be described as the mental ability to analyse objectively the available information and thereby make an appropriate judgment based on reasoning. Analysis involves breaking down of information into its constituent elements or small bits. Analytical ability enables a person to isolate and identify the different components of any given argument. This ability helps in making an in-depth study of any product, process or situation. Analysis clarifies inter-relationships among different variables and the sequence of a set of ideas. It is an important component of creative thinking as well. We can acquire knowledge by engaging in critical thinking. It helps us in improving our theories. We can strengthen our arguments using critical thinking. Critical thinking can also be used to enhance work processes and improve social institutions.

Critical thinking further involves the evaluation of sources, including data, facts, observable phenomena and research findings. Successful critical thinkers, based on analysis and evaluation of information, draw reasonable conclusions. They can now discriminate between details that are more useful and others that are trivial while solving a particular problem or making a decision.

In the knowledge age, critical thinking abilities are sought-after the most by employers in industry and business. They prefer candidates who are able to evaluate a situation using logical thinking and thus arrive at the best solution. Such critical thinkers take independent decisions by systematically analysing and identifying worthwhile details to solve given problems. Critical thinking generally involves understanding inter-relationships between ideas, determining their importance and relevance, identifying errors or inconsistencies in one's own reasoning, approaching every problem systematically and in a consistent manner, building and simultaneously making an appraisal of the arguments and always reflecting on the beliefs, values and assumptions made in the process.

Importance of Critical Thinking

Every human being requires clear and rational thinking ability to successfully accomplish any activity in life. In every walk of life and livelihood, critical thinking plays a very important role. In each and every career the ability to solve emerging problems systematically using critical thinking is considered an asset. The emerging knowledge economy is characterised by rapid changes. It is driven by ICT. Hence for sustaining and developing the economy, such trainable and intellectually flexible workforce is required who have the analytical ability and can effectively synthesise from diverse knowledge sources to efficiently solve emerging problems. In other words, people with good critical thinking are welcome in workplaces undergoing fast technological changes.

Since critical thinking basically means clear and systematic analytical thinking, it enables one to express ideas rationally and improve the ability to comprehend news, views, ideas and concepts. We are aware that creative thinking concerns with generating new ideas. But these ideas must be useful and relevant for a creative solution. Therefore, ideas need to be evaluated, and best ones are to be selected. Sometimes ideas may require due modification or improvement. This process, as we can see, requires critical thinking. Therefore, critical thinking is an essential part of creative thinking as well. In life, there are instances when one has to reflect on their values, decisions and actions to introduce correctives and justify or modify as needed. Self-evaluation of this kind requires the ability of critical thinking.

As a matter of fact, critical thinking is an important and essential life skill for extrapolation in social sciences, experimentation in sciences and to contribute effectively as a critical and independent thinker in a liberal democratic set-up.

In this context, it will be worthwhile to quote from the National Education Policy 2020, which emphasises that "Indeed, with the quickly changing employment and global ecosystem, it is becoming increasingly important that children not only learn but learn how to learn. Education must, thus, move towards less content and more towards learning about how to think critically and solve problems, how to be creative and multi-disciplinary, and how to innovate, adapt, and absorb new material in novel and changing fields".

Creative Thinking

Creative thinking refers to the ability to see things, problems and situations from different and new perspectives. It is directed towards finding new and unusual ways for solving problems. Guilford and his associates identified the abilities believed to be most relevant for creative thinking as sensitivity to problems, fluency of ideas, flexibility, originality, reorganisation and improvisation. Torrance (1967) stated that the old myth about creativity being the function of superior genes and 'talent will come out' has exploded. Now researchers and theorists have established that every individual is creative to a greater or lesser degree and that the development of creativity cannot be left to chance.

Creative thinking, in essence, is a way of problem-solving and where there is no problem-solving involved, it is a way of using one's ideas for productive purposes. Every child can be trained to use their mind creatively. At least five levels of creative thinking have been identified. These are (a) expressive level, (b) productive level, (c) inventive level, (d) innovative level, and (e) emergent level. With most children, we can work up to the second level at least, and it is worth doing. Quite a number of them could also work at the third level. What the teacher has to do in this context is to first learn to respond to the creative needs of the learner and then be ready to go beyond textbooks, the classroom, and the prescribed syllabus.

Developing Creative Potential

If the development of creativity is not to be left to chance, we have to find out some means of developing creative potential. Few pertinent questions in this context are, 'Can the educational system develop, nurture and achieve a truly creativity-stimulating environment?' Is creativity simply a result of preparation, incubation, inspiration, or can it be learned?' As a point of fact, many universities today offer courses in creative problem-solving. Many companies and corporations conduct creative problem-solving programmes for their engineers and management personnel.

The oldest but simple and most effective means of generating creative ideas is 'attribute listing'. A teacher, while using this method, asks the learners to itemise important attributes of a product. Each attribute thus listed is considered a source of potential change or improvement (Sen Gupta, 1984). Learners identify and systematically change the attributes and thus learn to improve objects, materials, manufacturing processes, cost, and marketability of the product. Similar to attribute listing, 'morphological synthesis' is another procedure in which learners list as many characteristics as possible of the given problem. They also list specific values for each. Taking one value at a time, several possible combinations are worked out. This technique is useful in generating a large variety of ideas in a short span of time to change or modify an object or gadget. Some of these combinations are likely to bring out a new product.

'Brainstorming' is yet another method to encourage the production of large number of ideas freely without any inhibition. The basic premise in brainstorming is that greater the number of ideas, greater is the chances of finding useful ones. Learners may even try to combine two or more ideas for forming newer set of ideas. In such sessions, participants accept all sorts of ideas and do not criticise even the most farfetched ones. 'Synectics' is another technique in which an approach based on direct analogy or personal analogies is followed. It can be used in its simplified form to stimulate the imagination of learners. A new but potential approach is that of 'bionics'. In this structure, functions and mechanisms of animals are carefully studied. Information thus gathered is used to gain design information for analogous manmade systems.

Schools and colleges, in this manner, should design methods and procedures to make learners think independently and find innovative solutions to day-to-day problems.

Conclusion

In the twenty-first century knowledge society, therefore, focus of learning in schools and colleges will have to be on creativity and innovation. Strong foundation of critical and creative thinking will be important because emerging problems are likely to require novel and hitherto untried approaches for their satisfactory solution. We are aware that every skill requires constant practice to gain proficiency; so also in the case of critical and creative thinking. Students should be regularly exposed to situations and problems requiring both these types of thinking skills. This need has been duly acknowledged by the first policy document of the twenty-first century. "It (National Education Policy 2020) believes that the purpose of education is to develop good human beings-capable of rational thought and action, possessing compassion and empathy, courage and resilience, scientific temper and creative imagination, with sound ethical moorings and values". The policy emphasises "on creativity and critical thinking (to encourage logical decision-making and innovation)".

References

Sen Gupta, M. (1984) Psychology of Engineering Creativity. New Delhi: Cosmo Publications.

Torrance, E.P. (1967) The Minnesota Studies of creative Behavior: National and International Extensions *The Journal of Creative Behaviour*, 1 (2), 137–154.

GOI, MHRD. National Education Policy 2020, 6.8, Page 24. New Delhi.

GOI, MHRD. National Education Policy 2020, 4.41, page 18. New Delhi.

GOI, MHRD (2020) National Education Policy, 0.3, page 3, New Delhi.

Index

Q

R

S

T